Consp

MW00904462

Conspiracy Theories – The Most Famous Conspiracies Including: The New World Order, False Flags, Government Cover-ups, CIA, & FBI

information contained within this document, including, but not limited to, errors, omissions, or inaccuracies.

Table of Contents

Introduction

Are things really as simple as they seem? Should you believe everything that popular media tells you? Some things are not really meant to be taken at face value, especially if they leave you with doubts in your mind. For most people, conspiracy theories are tall tales from the minds of crazy lunatics, but if you look closely, most of them do have at least some basis in fact, so it is unwise to dismiss them immediately.

In this book, you will learn about the most popular and most resilient conspiracy theories. The fact that these theories persist until today should be more than enough to make people think twice about their authenticity. Some of these stories may seem a bit far-fetched, and may even make you doubt what is actually real, but do keep an open mind and become more skeptical before passing judgment.

By the end of this book, you may learn to be more critical about the news that you hear. You will become more skeptical and learn to question things when you are not satisfied with the available answers.

Chapter 1 – The New World Order

Secret societies abound in the world of conspiracy theories, but arguably the most influential, and probably the scariest one of all is the New World Order.

Who controls the operations of the countries of the world? Most people will tell you that it's the Presidents and Prime Ministers of the countries of the world who are responsible for maintaining peace on Earth, but what if I told you that the ruling class came from just one gene pool? Would you believe me if I told you that a small group of highly influential and incredibly wealthy individuals are pulling the strings behind the scenes, and everything happening right now is part of their own secret agenda? It sounds a bit crazy, but there are quite a lot of people who firmly believe in this so-called New World Order.

The end times

Actually, besides the theory about its existence, other conspiracy theories make mention of the New World Order. One of the most intriguing stories is that the New World Order is the culmination of the story of the End Time as mentioned in the Holy Bible. In the book of Revelations, there's a mention of a tyrannical world government that will herd and control all of the remaining people on earth.

As many biblical prophecies have already been fulfilled, many believe the story of End Time will also prove to be true. The story of End Time predicts perilous times at the hands of the "antichrist", which many now assume to be the New World Order. The Holy Bible heeds many warning signs of end times, many of which have begun to reveal themselves. The elimination of cash and heavy reliance on credit and debit cards is one of the most prominent signs. The bible's predictions suggest that the "beast" system or the New World Order would enforce their rule by preventing access to money to those who refuse to comply. This is easily achieved with credit and debit cards since those in power could simply shut off access to individuals' accounts.

Another sign of end times is the recent increase in violent protests, riots, and mass hysteria. The End Time story states that God will eventually, "destroy them which destroy the earth". Along with mass violence and war, mankind has quite recently taken to destroying the earth by mowing down forests, polluting the air with toxins and chemicals, and causing entire species of animals to go extinct.

A very specific sign of end times is the increase in knowledge. In the past 50 years, technology has advanced more than ever. People all around the world can now fit more information in their pocket than could fit in an entire library 100 years ago.

As the economy continues to collapse, and war, famine, and strife envelope the world, the bible suggests the New World Order will fool the world's people by offering a "solution" to the nation's problems. Their "solution" however, will end up leading to the end of days. Though it may seem extreme to some, more concerning biblical prophecies seem to be fulfilled each and every day, making it incredibly hard to ignore the possibility of a totalitarian government forming in our society right under our noses.

Freemasons

The New World Order is also thought to be connected to another secret society, the Freemasons, and many even think that they are one and the same. One of the conspiracy theories linking the Freemasons and the New World Order stretches as far back as the founding of the United States of America. According to this theory, the Founding Fathers, namely George Washington and Benjamin Franklin (both Freemasons), incorporated Masonic symbols into the Great Seal of the United States, in the One-dollar bill, and in various structures and in the city grid system of the Nation's Capital, all of which is in preparation of the coming of the New World Order.

Freemasonry, or Masonry originates from local fraternities of stonemasons in the early 16th-17th centuries. As Freemasonry began expanding, its ties to the New World Order became more and more apparent. Since 1776 at least 14 United States Presidents have been Freemasons. Along with George Washington and Benjamin Franklin, fellow Presidential Freemasons include Andrew Jacksons, James K. Polk, James Buchanan, Andrew Johnson, James A. Garfield, and most recently, Gerald R. Ford. Not to mention, these Masonic Presidents were not alone, since at least 18 Vice Presidents, and 40 Supreme Court Judges since 1776 were also active Freemasons.

Many conspiracies have surrounded the Freemasons since the earliest days of their existence. In 1826, William Morgan mysteriously disappeared after threatening to uncover Masonic secrets. The writer planned to reveal the information in his upcoming book. Consequently, the Freemasons set fire to William Morgan's publishers. Shortly after, Morgan was arrested for an outstanding debt, and upon his release, was immediately rearrested. During his second imprisonment, a man claiming to be Morgan's friend came to pay his bail. After that second release, Morgan was never seen again.

Conspiracy researcher, William Guy Carr brought to light an 1871 letter written by Army General, Albert Pike, that prophesized three world wars. Rumored to be on display at the British Museum in London, the letter was an exchange between Pike and revolutionary leader Giuseppe Mazzini. Pike explained to Mazzini, a known supporter of a unified Italy and United States of Europe, that the first world war would overthrow Czars and build a "fortress of atheistic communism". He wrote that the second world war would turn the Fascists against the Zionists, and finally, the third world war would be fought between the Islamists and Zionists, after which, Lucifer would rise to power.

The Judeo-Masonic conspiracy details a union between the Jewish religion and the Freemasons in order to eliminate all non-Jews, or goyim, from the Earth. This conspiracy originates from the *Protocols of the Elders of Zion*, which was published in the year 1905 by Sergei Nilus in Russia. The protocols state that the Jews are the power behind Freemasonry, and simply use the fraternities as a cover.

One incredibly evident conspiracy surrounding Freemasonry is their irrefutable link to the occult. Many Masonic symbols and rituals can be easily traced back to Pagan roots. For example, the Masonic holiday, St. John's Day, falls closely around the time of the Winter Solstice, a primarily Pagan holiday. It is heavily insinuated by many Masonic texts that the fraternities in fact worship Satan, or Lucifer. The Freemasons have been tied to Satanism since the early 1800's. Their most recognizable symbol, the double headed eagle, has actually been proven to instead represent the ancient bird of Egypt, a Phoenix. Until 1841, the Presidential Seal depicted a Phoenix, rather than the eagle represented today. It is believed the Egyptians saw the Phoenix as a representation of Lucifer, making the ancient bird a strangely suspicious choice for the notable Masonic symbol. Horatio Greenough's iconic statue of George Washington depicts the president in a pose oddly similar to that of Baphomet, the most universal portrayal of Satan.

The Illuminati

One cannot talk about the New World Order without mentioning one of the most mysterious secret societies of all, the Illuminati. Conspiracy theorists believe that the Illuminati, whose founding dates back centuries, is responsible for many of the world's most significant events. For instance, in the 18th century, physicist John Robison and Jesuit priest Augustin Barruel believed that the Illuminati was responsible for instigating the French Revolution and starting the Reign of Terror, and if you think about it, they do have the capability of doing both.

The belief of the Illuminati, also called the Enlightened Ones, is that they are the only ones who have the intellect and the power to establish and control a centralized world government.

Many conspiracy theorists believe the Illuminati are not only responsible for perpetuating past tragedies, but the most recent ones as well. The collapse of the Twin Towers on 9/11 has been said to be orchestrated entirely by the Illuminati. The 9/11 attacks were a defining moment for the U.S. Government, allowing them to wage war against so-called "terrorism". Waging war meant engaging funding, which was likely the Illuminati's motivation. The 9/11 debacle was even predicted in an April, 2001 episode of the Cartoon Network series, *Johnny Bravo*. In the episode entitled, "Chain Gang Johnny", a movie poster can be seen depicting the Twin Towers in flames with the words "Coming Soon" plastered over it. The poster is shown as the two main characters discuss symbolism. This was likely an incredibly dark, tongue-in-cheek move made by the Illuminati.

Along with their ability to orchestrate national tragedies, and manipulate global governments, the Illuminati is said to control the pharmaceutical industry. It is believed that the Illuminati discovered a cure for cancer years ago, but continue to withhold it from scientists to this day. Cancer is one of the world's most lethal killers, so why would the Illuminati purposely prevent the medical community from attaining a cure? Much like the motivation behind most of their sinister plans, the answer is money. If the Illuminati truly controls the world's pharmaceuticals, a cure for cancer would mean a huge loss in revenue from cancer drugs, chemotherapy, and other unreasonably expensive cancer treatments. As long as the world's people remain sick and in need of prolonged medical treatment, the more the Illuminati profit.

The assassination of John F. Kennedy is another event that is rumored to have been carried out by the Illuminati. It is said President Kennedy was attempting to expose the Illuminati and their twisted web, which lead to the organization silencing him once and for all.

Politicians and government workers are not the only people under the suspicion of being a part of this elite group. Well-known, beloved celebrities such as Madonna, Kanye West,

Michael Jackson, Lady Gaga, and Bill Gates have all been linked to the Illuminati. Beyoncé Knowles appeared to be flashing Illuminati hand signals during her 2013 Super Bowl half-time performance, while singer, Rihanna featured a flurry of Illuminati imagery in her "What Now" music video. Throughout the years, the Illuminati have become thoroughly integrated in pop culture, likely recruiting celebrities because of their familarity and influence in regular society. One of the most prominent Illuminati conspiracies surrounding a celebrity, is the one that encompasses Elvis Presley. Often referred to as "The King" of the music world, many believe Presley was an Illuminati pawn who requested "out of the business". Some say the Illuminati agreed to Presley's request, killing off the famous Elvis persona and allowing him to live out the rest of his days as a man named John Burrows. Others believe the Illuminati sent a doctor, George Nichopoulos, to inflict a slow decline in Presley's health which would eventually kill him. The purpose of prolonging his death was to attract attention from fans, boosting his record sales through the roof upon his death, leaving the Illuminati to relish in the profits.

One interesting theory was discovered by detailed research of the most influential rumored Illuminati members and their bloodlines. Upon in-depth studying of their ancestry, George W. Bush was found to be a distant cousin of Abraham Lincoln, along with Princess Diana of Wales, Dick Cheney, John Kerry, and even Marilyn Monroe and Tom Hanks. The evidence that all of these powerful, well-known people are related by blood seems like a peculiar coincidence, one that can be easily explained by a long line of Illuminati unions and breeding.

Despite extensive research, it is nearly impossible to prove or disprove the existence and severity of these supposed elite groups and their influence over society. Along with the aforementioned instances, there are many other conspiracy theories linked to the New World Order and the Illuminati, but let's stop this discussion for now so we can move on to the others on our list.

Chapter 2 – The JFK Assassination

On November 22, 1963, in Dallas, Texas, a lone gunman assassinated President John F. Kennedy, or so it seemed. It was one of the darkest days in the history of the United States, and even though the authorities captured shooter, Lee Harvey Oswald, there were too many inconsistencies so that conspiracy theorists have had a field day with it.

On that fateful day, even Jacqueline (Jackie) Kennedy was right next to her husband. Although Mrs. Kennedy did not often accompany her husband during his political travels, on that November day she was sitting right next to him in the Lincoln convertible which would prove to be the President's place of death.

Apart from Jackie, Texas Governor John Connelly was inside the car as well. All three of them were greeting the crowd on the both sides of the road. Vice President Lyndon Johnson also accompanied the President, but he was in a different car, a few vehicles behind Kennedy's.

At exactly 12:30 pm, three shots were fired in the direction of the President's Lincoln, as the car was passing by the School Book Depository Building. The bullets inflicted fatal wounds to the President and seriously injured the Governor.

Only a couple of hours after the assassination, Vice President Johnson was sworn into office aboard Air Force One situated in Dallas. The entire ceremony, if one could call it that, took seven minutes after which the airplane departed for Washington. Among the thirty people who witnessed Johnson taking the oath was Jacqueline Kennedy, still wearing the blood-stained clothes.

Upon returning to Washington, Johnson declared November 25th as a day of national mourning. On that day, the late President Kennedy was buried at the Arlington National Cemetery with full military honors, and hundreds of thousands of people following the entire sad event out on the streets or in their homes.

To this day, the circumstances surrounding Kennedy's death remain unclear despite the fact that the police captured Lee Harvey Oswald within two hours of the assassination. There are several theories which insist that Oswald had an accomplice during the very act, and even more of those claiming that he was acting on the orders coming from the high-up state officials and the CIA.

Who was Lee Harvey Oswald?

Oswald, who was born in New Orleans in 1939, was a former U.S. Marine. He served for three years and when he was discharged in 1959, he left for the Soviet Union. Since his plans to become a citizen there did not work out, despite having a Soviet wife, he came back to the States in 1962.

According to official evidence, upon his return to the US, Oswald had become involved in a number of activities against the Government and its officials. He was suspected in an assassination attempt on a former U.S. Army General, Edwin Walker, earlier in 1963. Allegedly, he made a trip to Mexico City in September, trying to obtain a visa to go to Cuba or return to the Soviet Union, but he was again unsuccessful.

In October, he got a job at the Texas School Book Depository, the building from which he perpetrated the assassination later that month. After the President was shot, Oswald also killed a police officer who was questioning him, then he was arrested some thirty minutes after that.

The very next day, on November 24th, the police were preparing to transfer Lee Harvey Oswald to a more secure jail. Not surprisingly, there was a huge crowd in front of the Dallas police station, from regular people to members of the media. A man named Jack Ruby managed to smuggle in a gun and opened fire on Oswald, afflicting upon him a fatal wound with a single shot. He was immediately arrested and claimed the motive for the murder was rage caused by the assassinator's act.

The theory of the second gunman

The conspiracy theory revolving around the purported second gunman stemmed from the conclusion of the United States House Select Committee on Assassination (HSCA) in 1979 that another gunman besides Oswald shot at the President at the exact same time. The HSCA failed to identify whom this second person is, which led to the discrediting of their findings.

The original HSCA report stated that witnesses testified hearing four gunshots, and since the rifle that Oswald used could only shoot two rounds from his position at the Book Depository building, the committee believed that there is a possibility that there was a second gunman stationed atop the grassy knoll beside the parade route.

CIA cover-up

A 2013 CIA report that was declassified in 2014 stated that former Director John McCone purposely withheld information from the Warren Commission, which was tasked by then President Lyndon Johnson to spearhead the investigation of the JFK assassination.

According to the author of the report, CIA Historian David Robarge, Director McCone and other top officials of the agency were part of a cover-up aimed at keeping the HSCA focused on what they believed was "the best truth", which is that Lee Harvey Oswald acted on his own. This seemed to ignore the fact that the Warren Commission received hundreds of witness accounts that they heard gunshots coming from the grassy knoll; and some even claimed to see smoke. However, Director McCone insisted that Oswald acted alone, and he told the CIA to provide only "passive, reactive and selective" assistance to the HSCA.

This led to multiple inconsistencies in the Warren Commission report, the biggest of which is the "single bullet" theory. The report mentioned that a single bullet hit and killed President Kennedy, which in itself seems to break every rule of Physics. How could a single bullet enter through the back of JFK's neck, hit Texas Governor John Connally square in the back, exit his chest, and still have enough energy to embed itself in the governor's thigh? It was preposterous to claim that a half-inch bullet could have enough force to pierce through all that clothing and flesh, and yet the Warren Commission stuck by its theory.

The fact that Lee Harvey Oswald was also assassinated a day after his arrest only made the conspiracy theory about the CIA cover-up seem more plausible. How was it possible for an armed gunman to get near Oswald, who at the time was surrounded by a dozen police officers and news reporters? Is it possible that the CIA orchestrated everything to silence Oswald?

President Johnson's role

A poll conducted in 2003 revealed that 20% of Americans believe that President Lyndon Johnson was directly involved in Kennedy's assassination and the aftermath. Even Jackie Kennedy, the late President's wife, believed that Johnson was responsible for what happened on that dark day in November. But the question is, what could have possibly motivated Johnson to take such a step?

Jackie believed it was all an elaborate plot that was designed to enable Johnson to become the president himself. According to some sources, the only reason Johnson was even in a position of power and had an opportunity to become the next president was because he was blackmailing President Kennedy, forcing JFK to name him the Vice President.

However, was the hunger for power of one man enough? Could Johnson have orchestrated and put in motion this entire plan on his own?

On October 11, 1963, JFK issued the National Security Action Memorandum 263, which stated that 1,000 of the military personnel were to be withdrawn from Vietnam by the end of the year. Naturally, not everyone was thrilled with this decision.

One of the very first things Johnson did after ascending to power, as early as November 26th, was to issue the Executive Order 273, which effectively invalidated the NSAM 263. Many believe that this was one of the main reasons behind the assassination, and that Lyndon Johnson was just the puppet in the hands of real power and those who did not like the idea of withdrawing troops from Vietnam. By leaving the troops where they were, the military industry could keep spending vast amounts of money on the war that was clearly impossible to win.

Another factor that added backing to this theory was the fact that Johnson was very quick to remove all of Kennedy's belongings from the White House. As early as 9 am the next day, everything that remained of the late president was moved out.

In addition to all of this more or less circumstantial evidence, there was a partial print found at the place from which the shots were fired. For a while, the identity behind the partial remained a mystery, but it was eventually connected to the man named Malcolm Wallace who was a known acquaintance and associate of President Johnson.

Wallace was first arrested in 1951, for the murder of John Douglas Kinser, who was believed to have had affairs with Johnson's sister Josefa and Wallace's wife. Despite the overwhelming evidence, Wallace was found guilty of first-degree murder and received a shocking 5 year suspended sentence.

Malcolm Wallace was indicted in several other murders over the years, including the murder of Johnson's sister Josefa. However, there was never enough evidence or will to pursue this matter further, and Lyndon Johnson ran for the presidential office in 1964 and went on to win the election. He completed his term, retired from politics and moved to his ranch in Texas.

Other probable reasons for JFK's assassination

One of the probable reasons why the CIA wanted Kennedy killed was because he removed its then director, Allen Dulles, because of the travesty that was the Bay of Pigs invasion. After that tragedy, Kennedy reportedly said that he would start dissolving the CIA, or at least split it into multiple divisions.

Another probable reason why the CIA would have been behind the JFK assassination might be that the President had a secret correspondence with then Soviet leader, Nikita Khrushchev right after the terrifying Cuban missile crisis. The CIA got even more enraged when it learned that JFK was planning to talk and sign a peace treaty with Fidel Castro, which the agency had been planning to take over ever since the nuclear scare.

Every day, people are uncovering new evidence that may solve the mystery as to who really killed President John F. Kennedy. However, conspiracy theorists are still unconvinced that the answer will come in their lifetime.

What to believe?

Amongst the vast amount of different conspiracy theories surrounding Kennedy's assassination, partnered with a lot of circumstantial evidence and some really outlandish theories, it is hard to know what to believe.

There is certainly a considerable amount of evidence to make you question whether everything was revealed in this particular case. It is hard to believe that one man alone could coordinate and execute a plan to assassinate a U.S. president with such success. He would have to be extremely lucky to go undetected and position himself perfectly to perform the shooting.

Beyond that, however, it is hard to state what the truth is. Was President Johnson really involved and to what extent? There are different indications to this effect but it is hard to know for sure, and people in high profile cases are prone to rumors. So, one should always take everything with a pinch of salt.

Similarly, it is easy to believe that the CIA had involvement in the matter just because people love to get the Agency involved in everything. Of course, their involvement is far from impossible, but at this point in time, it is hard to say anything with any real degree of certainty.

Chapter 3 – The Moon Landing

One of the crowning glories of the United States was when the country won the "Space Race" against the Soviets by being the first to put human beings on the moon. However, a small, persistent group of conspiracy theorists do not believe that the moon landing actually happened, and that it was all an elaborate hoax filmed in a Hollywood sound stage.

In the 1960s, scientists were just figuring out how to build an efficient computer; even the now commonplace computer mouse was still in development back then, which seems more than enough reason to doubt that NASA had the capability to send a team to the moon and actually broadcast it live on TV.

Besides the seemingly impossible technical hurdles that NASA somehow overcame, there were a couple more inconsistencies with the actual moon landing footage.

The American flag fluttering in a windless atmosphere

One of the most puzzling things about the moon landing was how it was possible for the American flag to flutter about, as if being blown by the wind, even though there was no air on the surface of the moon? NASA claimed that the flag was not fluttering at all; it was just crumpled up from being in storage for so long, and it was only settling in place, hence the movement.

Shadows did not line up properly

In one of the photographs taken by the astronauts, the shadows were not running parallel to each other, which is something that is only possible when there are more than one light source hitting the targets. On the moon, the only source of light that can cast shadows on the surface is the sun, but in some of the photographs that the astronauts took on the surface of the moon, the shadows were skewed, some are even running into each other. It's almost as if there were multiple lights in their location, just like in a movie set.

The "C" rock

One of the most damning pieces of evidence that the moon landing was a hoax is the famous "C" rock. In one of the photographs supposedly taken by the astronauts, one rock had a perfect letter C carved into it. Rocks and stones do have pits on their surface due to natural erosion; but what are the odds of erosion forming a perfect letter C? It seems as if one of the "stage hands" forgot to turn over one of the rocks to hide the obvious prop marks.

NASA, in an effort to debunk this claim, stated that the letter C was just a stray hair that got into the film during development. It was quite unlikely that NASA, with all of their meticulous planning, would be careless enough to let a stray hair get into the film.

The Van Allen radiation belt

One of the reasons why conspiracy theorists refuse to believe that the moon landing ever happened is because of the Van Allen radiation belt. Everyone knew that even the slightest exposure to radiation would result in sickness and maybe even death, and that's only from radiation sources on earth. The radiation in the Van Allen belt is hundreds, if not thousands of times stronger than anything that can be found on our planet's surface, and yet, three people were able to go through it without any adverse effects whatsoever.

NASA claimed that the Apollo space craft was covered in aluminum, which greatly lessened the amount of radiation that got inside it. They also claimed that the astronauts were only in the Van Allen belt for a short amount of time, not enough to do too much damage. The details are actually a bit sketchy because the aluminum cover should not have been enough to repel a huge amount of radiation, and the astronauts were reportedly in the Van Allen belt for an hour and a half, which is actually quite a long time.

The lunar module not leaving a mark

People are familiar with the photographs of the astronauts' footprints on the lunar surface. Every little detail of the soles of their boots were evident on the prints; the astronauts actually describe the dust on the moon like fine, wet sand. Here's the thing: why didn't the lunar module, which was obviously heavier than the astronauts, leave a mark?

Upon closer inspection of the pictures of the lunar module, you will see that the landing gear did not even leave a small crater on the surface. If one person was heavy enough to leave a footprint on the lunar surface, why didn't tons of high tech equipment even leave a mark. It's almost as if the lunar module was already in place even before the "astronauts" walked on the moon's surface.

The duplicate backdrops

There are two photographs from two separate Apollo 15 missions supposedly taken from different locations on the moon, but upon closer inspection, you will see that the mountain ranges in the background were completely identical. How could this have been possible when the two moon missions supposedly were miles apart from each other. The camera needed to be in the exact same angle in both pictures for this to even make sense, but the odds of that happening in real life are slim to none. The only possible explanation for this phenomenon is that they used the same backdrop to take the two pictures.

Camera crosshairs miraculously went behind the objects

The cameras used in the moon missions supposedly had crosshairs imprinted on the lens to aid the astronauts who are taking the pictures. When the photographs are printed, these crosshairs should go on top of the images in the picture. However, in some of the photographs that came from multiple lunar missions, the crosshairs were suspiciously behind the objects in the foreground.

There was one picture where the American flag somehow got in front of the camera's crosshairs, and there were some where parts of the lunar rover were covering the guide lines. Conspiracy theorists believe that NASA just superimposed the images over pictures of barren landscapes.

Plenty of other inconsistencies plague the moon landing, but NASA is still tight-lipped on the issue. If they have been able to keep this a secret for this long, it is quite possible that the truth will never be known.

Lack of stars

One particularly compelling argument amongst conspiracy theorists is the complete lack of stars present in both photos and videos of the moon landing. Despite the distance, clouds, and light pollution that occurs on Earth, we are still able to see stars with the naked eye, and photograph them. Stars are noticeable even in low quality photographs.

On the moon, there are no clouds, and no light pollution, so why didn't any show up in the footage? Conspiracy theorists believe it would have been impossible for NASA to map out the exact locations of the stars around the moon, and therefore left them out. NASA's only justification for the lack of stars is that the quality of the photos washed them out. The idea that an organization capable of traveling to the moon and broadcasting it on live television did not have the technology to capture a photo of the stars is very odd.

The Stanley Kubrick theory

The year before the moon landing in 1968, famed director Stanley Kubrick released the science fiction classic, *2001: A Space Odyssey*. The groundbreaking film produced a stunning, and realistic looking display of space travel. Because Kubrick was able to convey incredible visuals of space in the film, some conspiracy theorists believe Kubrick was hired by the government to stage the moon landing. Other's believe Kubrick had been hired years before the moon landing, and

2001: A Space Odyssey, was simply a test run before actually staging the event.

Conspiracists believe that Stanley Kubrick slipped evidence that proves this theory into his other notable films. For example, in one scene the child in the film is wearing an Apollo 11 shirt. Theorists also reference the main character's famous line, "All work and no play makes Jack a dull boy", saying the word "all" is meant to be interpreted as "A11", or Apollo 11. The evidence here is very far reaching, however, if the moon landing was in fact a staged, Hollywood hoax, Stanley Kubrick would be a likely choice for its direction.

Chapter 4 – Was The Holocaust a Conspiracy?

According to the mainstream history and ample evidence from the World War Two period, the Holocaust was one of the biggest tragedies that a single nation has ever had to endure. It is estimated that some six million Jews were killed during the Nazi rule of Germany.

It was a systematic endeavor with the ultimate goal of wiping out the entire Jewish population residing in Europe at that time. Since the total number amounted to around 9 million, Nazis were able to put two-thirds of their plan in action before they were finally stopped.

However, not everyone agrees with the mainstream history. There are some voices out there claiming that the Holocaust is, in fact, a Jewish conspiracy. There is no denying that the Nazis systematically persecuted and executed Jews during the period between 1941 - 1945, but are reported numbers truly accurate?

The Holocaust Revisionism

The movement whose members and supporters claim that these reported numbers are excessive and exaggerated is widely known as The Holocaust Revisionism. They maintain that the actual proof to back up these claims is practically non-existent and often call the Holocaust "the greatest conspiracy theory ever devised in history."

The revisionists stand firm in their belief that the entire concept was an invention of Jewish extremists who refuse any debate on the topic and are not open to any modifications of their original claims. Allegedly, some people were even imprisoned to silence their voices and stop them from talking about real numbers.

What is the Revisionism based on?

Holocaust skeptics base their convictions on the lack of physical evidence to support the claims of the systematic genocide and six million victims. While the notorious gas chambers are often mentioned as the number one tool for executing Jews, according to them, not a single performed autopsy determined zyklonB (cyanide) to be the cause of death.

Furthermore, there is not a single official document which proves the existence of this grand scheme to kill the Jews in Europe. The entire theory is mostly based on the eyewitness accounts of war camp survivors which often contradict each other.

The only other witnesses, German soldiers who served as guards in these camps, have also been silenced effectively because if they try to claim that things did not happen the way they are being presented, they would be guilty of the "Holocaust denial."

How the Holocaust came to be

According to revisionists, the concept of the Holocaust was created by Jews in control of the mass media and the entertainment industry, most importantly Hollywood. They used their power and influence to indoctrinate regular people with the subject of the Holocaust. Thanks to these myths, the conspiracy theorists claim they were able to earn millions from movies, documentaries, and books dealing with the topic of Holocaust. On top of that, they also received vast amounts from European countries in the name of reparations.

Using these tactics, Jews were able to portray themselves as victims in the eyes of the world and used this position to perform aggressive actions against their enemies. Anyone who did not agree with their views was automatically deemed "anti-Semitic" and demonized as a Nazi.

Examining death camps

Of six camps that supposedly had the gas chambers, all six were situated in the parts of Poland occupied by the Soviet forces. A German chemist, Rudolf Germar, performed a detailed analysis of Auschwitz, looking for the proof to confirm or deny the existence of gas chambers. His work proved that it was virtually impossible for gas chambers to have existed in this notorious death camp. The so-called "The Rudolf Report" contains around 500 pages and explains the science behind the gas chambers and much more.

In his report, Germar mostly focuses on the fact that the Nazis simply lacked the technical requirements to make gas chambers a feasible option for mass executions. With hydrogen cyanide being a very dangerous and extremely unstable poison, it was virtually impossible to use it on such a scale, in the Auschwitz environment, without putting at risk the lives of guards and other personnel there.

Dachau was the only camp that was not controlled by Soviets where there were claims of gas chambers being used. Later, however, it was admitted that gas chambers of Dachau were just a fabrication created by the U.S. media and that gas chambers were never used there.

In fact, the revisionists maintain, the main cause of death in the concentration camps were different diseases, primarily typhus. The overpopulated and overcrowded spaces of the camps were an excellent area for this vicious disease to flourish, taking away the lives of thousands.

Holocaust myth and mysteries

Many Holocaust skeptics reference the numerous mysteries surrounding the event when arguing its validity. For example, one of the Holocaust's more twisted rumors revolved around a Nazi woman named Ilse Koch, otherwise known as the "Bitch of Buchenwald". It had been said that Koch was responsible for crafting lampshades, and possibly other household items, out of human skin that had been taken from the Jews in the concentration camp. In 2012, the history channel released a documentary entitled Human Lampshade: A Holocaust Mystery. The documentary followed a man who'd found a bizarre lampshade in New Orleans following Hurricane Katrina that was said to be a dark relic of the Holocaust. After running numerous tests on the lampshade, results proved it was not made of human skin, but rather, animal skin. Holocaust skeptics say the lack of a human skin lampshade as evidence is a sign that the Holocaust may not have taken place.

Another example of this is the disappearance of the Die Blutfahne, or the "Blood Flag". The Die Blutfahne was one of the earliest symbols of the Nazi party and was used in many of their rituals. The last sighting of the flag was documented in October 1944. It has never been seen since. Other missing Holocaust relics include an automobile-sized globe from Adolf Hitler's office, and various art pieces. Though it is likely these articles were either destroyed or lost, these missing items make Holocaust skeptics all the wearier.

Just about any unsolved mystery related to the Holocaust causes skeptics to wonder why those orchestrating the event made careless mistakes and failed to tie up various loose ends. During the routine maintenance of a building inside Auschwitz in 2009, a group of historians discovered a piece of paper listing the names of 17 British soldiers. Each name had a check mark next to it. It remains unclear what became of these soldiers, and what the list was for.

In 1945, a Swedish business man named Raoul Wallenberg was arrested by the Soviets. Prior to his arrest, Wallenberg was responsible for providing more than 100,000 Jews with falsified paperwork that allowed them to escape concentration camps. Wallenberg also established numerous soup kitchens, hospitals, and safe houses for the escaped Jews in Budapest. Following his arrest, it is unknown what happened to Raoul Wallenberg. One set of Soviet documents stated Wallenberg died in 1947 of a heart attack, but this conflicts other documents that state Wallenberg was questioned for 16 hours, one week after his supposed death.

What to believe?

There is no denying that there were persecutions of Jews during World War Two. Even the revisionists themselves, apart from the most extreme ones, are not denying this. But are all the numbers and facts really accurate or have there been some "updates" to the facts in order to make them seem even more gruesome and despicable?

Everyone is free to believe what they want, of course, but the truth is that history is rarely simply black and white. Historical exaggerations have been proven time and time again since, as the old saying goes, history is written by the winners.

We will probably never know for sure how many Jews were actually killed intentionally during World War Two. Of course, the numbers don't make the crime any less meaningful nor do they serve as a justification for the concentration camps. However, were the exaggerations used to help with certain political and social agendas? It is quite possible.

In this sense, "The Rudolf Report" is a very interesting read. If you try to examine it with an open mind and without taking any sides, there are certainly some factors that raise questions about the legitimacy of particular claims.

The topic of Holocaust is a very sensitive one and even talking about it is almost certainly bound to cause controversy. However, as the people of the 21st century, we must not be afraid to seek the evidence and look for the facts, regardless of how "touchy" the subject in question might be.

Chapter 5 – The Vatican Conspiracy

During the Middle Ages, the Catholic Church, led by a pope residing in the Vatican, had control over most of Europe. The Vatican confirmed and crowned kings, blessed or denied important political marriages, gathered armies, and launched campaigns against the heathens. There is no doubt that the Church enjoyed great power in those days, as the Pope was widely believed to be God's spokesman on Earth and his decisions were not to be disputed.

The Middle Ages have long passed, and the Catholic church has no official political power anymore outside the Vatican. However, many believe that the Popes and Cardinals of the Vatican are pulling the strings behind the scenes and have a major influence in all important world events.

The number of conspiracy theories connected to the Vatican is too great to cover completely, but we will mention some of the more intriguing ones here.

The secret archives

The Vatican Secret Archives are a part of the Vatican Library, housing thousands of documents, letters, and books, mostly about the state affairs. There are undoubtedly some highly valuable and interesting documents kept there, such as the letters of Michelangelo Buonarroti. However, the conspiracy theorists claim that there is much more hidden than the Vatican officials are willing to admit.

Among the numerous documents that conspiracy theorists believe are kept in the Secret Archives are Jesus' family tree or even the evidence that he never existed. They believe that these papers are kept well-hidden and away from prying eyes because their revelation could shake the very foundations of the Catholic Church and weaken their power in the world.

The mystery is furthered by the fact that only four people in the world are allowed access to the Archives. These are four Cardinals who take care of this part of the library. It is unclear if even the pope himself is allowed to roam freely through the archives. Anyone who wants to gain access can only do so by requesting it beforehand and only if they ask for a particular document they know is stored there.

This setup is a perfect ground for conspiracy theorists to let their imagination take over and come up with all sorts of possibilities as to what could be found in there. Unquestionably, there must be some very interesting documents kept in there, but is there anything of such importance and gravity to shake the foundations of the Church?

Vatican and the New World Order

Another widely spread conspiracy theory claims that the Vatican has a prominent place in the New World Order. We've already mentioned this concept in the first chapter so we will not be revisiting that topic, but we will briefly discuss the role of Catholic Church in the entire matter as believed by the conspiracy theorists.

They believe, not without some evidence to support these claims, that the Catholic Church, through certain individuals, has a major influence and monetary interest in a number of big corporations and even the central bank itself.

This theory is founded on the fact that the Vatican clearly possesses a big treasure in different shapes and forms, and thus, the people that have control over it are probably using it to earn even more money and further the influence of the Church.

It is believed that it all started in 1962, with The Second Vatican Council, gathered by Pope John XXIII. The Council introduced some important changes to the internal structure of the Church, like the use of vernacular language in Mass instead of Latin. Another important change was the introduction of folk songs instead of Gregorian Chants. These, along with many other changes, would alter the face of the Church; which had remained unchanged for centuries before.

These changes coincided with the worldwide revolution that took place during the 1960s and this was no coincidence. The revolution was in part caused by these shifting views of the Church, making the religious laws "friendlier" to common people.

Many believe that The Second Vatican Council and its decisions were brought about by the influence of Masonic lobbies, which managed to infiltrate the Church and establish their positions.

From this point on, the Catholic Church embarked on the path to once again establish their power in the world and become an influential force, spreading their interests in all walks of life and business.

Third secret of Fatima

In 1917, Virgin Mary appeared to three shepherds in the Portuguese town of Fatima and shared with them three big secrets. The church officially recognized the Fatima event, and two of these secrets or prophecies were revealed during the 1940's. However, the Third Secret has never been revealed and has become a source of many myths and theories.

Finally, in 2000, Pope John Paul II published the Third Secret together with an explanation by the Cardinal at the time, Joseph Ratzinger, who would later become Pope Benedict XVI. The Secret contained some gloomy predictions for Popes and Bishops, revolving around persecution and murder.

The explanation by Cardinal Ratzinger was meant to reassure people that this was by no means a fixed prophecy of things to come, but rather a warning that should help the Church protect itself from such unpleasant possibilities.

However, after the Third Secret was revealed, claims appeared from the public that Ratzinger had, in fact, told a close friend that there was more to this prophecy than what was published. Some of these claims even went as far as to state that certain prophecies directly concerned the papacy of Pope Francis and some of his actions, which, some believed, encouraged heresies.

The official Vatican had to respond to charges of this magnitude, and Pope Benedict, the only Pope who abdicated from the papal throne in centuries, came out of his retirement, stating that these allegations were completely untrue and that there was nothing hidden about the Third Secret of Fatima.

Despite this statement, many remained convinced that it was all just part of a large conspiracy. Benedict XVI's abdication, or, as he called it, renunciation, certainly did not help break the suspicions.

The Shroud of Turin

The Shroud of Turin is said to be the cloth used to bury Jesus Christ following his crucifixion, though the authenticity of the burial cloth has been questioned over the course of many years. Assuming the Shroud of Turin is legitimate, conspiracy theorists and researchers believe the cloth shows evidence that Jesus was alive after the crucifixion. The Jesus Conspiracy, a book published in 1994, explains that the Vatican likely interfered with carbon dating of the shroud to make it appear fake. This is because, if Jesus Christ survived his crucifixion, the church's entire theology would be destroyed. The Vatican has vehemently denied interfering with the Shroud of Turin.

Jesus and Mary Magdalene

Although this is an old theory, it is one that never goes out of style. It was brought to the center of attention once again through the writings of Dan Brown. The basic premise behind it is that Jesus Christ was married to Mary Magdalene, and that the church hid this information because it allowed them to promote celibacy as the only acceptable lifestyle for their priests, among other things.

On top of that, with the Church existing for 2,000 years based on this premise, finding any evidence that Jesus was in fact married, or perhaps even had children with Mary Magdalene would shake the institution's very foundation. It is then easy to see where the interest in this theory came from.

If we examine the available evidence, there isn't much to sway us either way. The Biblical gospels are the earliest accounts of Jesus' life and these writings don't specifically mention the marriage either way. His wife is never mentioned, but it is also never explicitly stated that he didn't have one.

Given how detailed the gospels are about other important aspects of Christ's life, it does seem unlikely that a detail as important as him being married would be completely omitted in all four gospels. For some, this alone is evidence enough that Jesus could not have been married.

Others, however, take this as proof that he was in fact married. Every Jewish man from that period got married, it was a custom, a tradition, and practically a social norm. But, it was not a law. No man was forced to get married if they preferred the life of solitude, and while the others might not look kindly on such a decision, it was certainly an option. And Jesus was known to go against many other norms and traditions of his time if we are to believe the gospels.

On top of this, there is the historical evidence that there existed a fairly large group of Jews, called Essenes, who mostly stayed unmarried. These apocalyptical Jews were awaiting God's second coming to Earth and believed that they needed no wives in their lives. While Jesus' opinion on many matters differed from that of Essenes, he too belonged to the group of those awaiting and announcing the arrival of God's Kingdom on Earth.

Moving on, we come to the question why Mary Magdalene is the one who is believed to be Christ's wife? Jesus had come in contact with a number of females according to the gospels and this had a great effect on their lives. Granted, from what we can read, Mary Magdalene certainly had a special kind of relationship with Jesus.

She accompanied him on his travels, and it seems that she helped him financially. But other than a few references, gospels don't explain a lot about Mary Magdalene or her relationship with Jesus. The biggest highlight of this relationship is that it was her whom the resurrected Jesus first showed himself to, and she was the first to spread the joyful news to his disciples.

So, the Biblical Gospels don't reveal that much about the relationship either way and if there is anything to suggest the marriage, then it is the fact that the marriage was never mentioned. Even for those who want to believe this theory, there is very weak evidence at best.

But, there is a group of documents known as the non-canonical gospels. These are the writings that were not included in the Bible because they were not believed to be credible or authentic. Of course, for conspiracy theorists, this is a great reason to "cry wolf" because the only possible reason for them not to be included was because they were hiding some sinister secrets.

The fact is that non-canonical gospels mostly date from the second or third century AD. This means they were written well after the original gospels of Mathew, Mark, Luke, and John. The writers were thus people who were somewhat remote from the actual events described in the gospels.

Putting all that aside, what do these gospels tell us about Mary Magdalene and her relationship with Jesus? Despite what conspiracy theorists may want to believe, it is in fact very little. The oldest of these, the Gospel of Thomas, only makes two brief references to her, and one of them hardly indicates that there was any special kind of relationship between the two. If anything, it indicates that Jesus wanted to treat all of his disciples the same, both men and women, as his disciples whom he wanted to lead to the heavenly kingdom.

Other later writings, like the Gospel of Peter or The Dialogue of the Savior, also don't make any explicit reference to the marriage or even any special relationship between Jesus and Mary Magdalene. The latter document does portray her as someone with deep knowledge of spiritual realities, but that is all.

Later writings of the Gnostic Christians are known for taking a particular interest in Mary Magdalene. In The Gospel of Mary, she is referred to as the one that the Savior (Jesus) loved more than any other woman. In another part of The Gospel of Mary, one of the disciples makes the statement, saying that the Savior loved her more than them (the disciples).

Unlike the earlier writings, this gospel does seem to indicate a very special, close, and personal relationship between Jesus and Mary of Magdalene. The marriage as such is not mentioned, but this is plenty to fuel the beliefs of those insisting there was more to this relationship than what is described in canonical gospels.

The document that the conspiracy theorists cling to the most is The Gospel of Philip, which was most likely written in the second half of the third century. This gospel mentions that Mary Magdalene was always by Jesus' side and was "called his companion." On top of this, another section of this gospel makes a claim that Jesus loved her more than others and "used to kiss her on the mouth often."

Even The Gospel of Philip doesn't mention the marriage as such, and since the disciples were jealous of this special treatment Mary had, it seems to suggest that there was no marital bond between them. After all, they would surely understand that a man must pay special attention to his wife?

Those looking to uncover the truth must also understand that Gnostic gospels and other writings often used metaphors and strange expressions, so kissing in this sense doesn't have to be translated literally. It may indicate simply that Jesus spoke to her more often and revealed to her the truths that were hidden from others.

Aside from all these texts, there are also many who believe that Vatican libraries hide a lot more evidence about Jesus' marriage and (possibly) his children. The reason I've spent so many words explaining this in detail is that this seems to be a somewhat "hot" topic when it comes to conspiracy theories, and there may be quite a few people interested in what evidence exists.

To the best of anyone's knowledge, what is described here is pretty much all of it, at least in its main points. Whether there are some deep, dark secrets carefully stashed away in the vaults of the Vatican, none of us can know for sure. If they do exist, you can be pretty sure that someone like Dan Brown did not have access to them, so his writing is 99% fiction backed by some loose indications found in a few documents. This is not to say that Jesus was or wasn't married, but there is certainly not enough proof to back up the claim of his marriage to Mary Magdalene at this point.

Why Vatican?

These are just a few of the numerous conspiracy theories connected to the Vatican. The question arises, why are the Vatican and its officials such an interesting area for conspiracy theorists. What is it that makes that small city-state so mysterious?

First and foremost, this has been a place of numerous intrigues and conspiracies in the past. There is no doubt that as far as secrets go, the Catholic Church has had its fair share of them throughout the history. We don't have to go far back. If we remember the 1970's and the scandal that the Vatican bank was involved in, it becomes clear that even the Holy Seat has its "bad apples." In 2013, Nunzio Scarano, a Vatican accountant, was arrested for his part in a cash-smuggling scheme.

Apart from this, the Vatican has always been a secretive place. A number of big and small secrets have been stored away in the great libraries and halls of Rome, and when some of them come to the light of day, it is only natural for people to start wondering how much more there is that they are not aware of.

Of course, there is no denying that this is one of the centers of the world power, even if it does not show itself in the same way it did during the Middle Ages. All these factors combined make the imagination go wild, especially with people prone to believing in conspiracy theories.

What the real truth is and which of these theories have merits, we might never find out. Certain bits and pieces appear from time to time, but they are certainly not enough to create a full picture either way.

Chapter 6 – Area 51

The infamous Area 51 has probably been the source of more conspiracy theories than any other place on earth, including the Bermuda Triangle.

Area 51 is the military base located some 80 miles outside Las Vegas, Nevada, and every year this place attracts a huge number of visitors who come as close as they can to the base, hoping to find some evidence of the aliens who supposedly visited our planet.

The mystery of Area 51

Area 51 is not just an ordinary military base. It is, in fact, a testing ground for the development of experimental weapons and aircraft. Because of this fact alone, it is covered in a veil of mystery and secrecy, as no one is allowed to come close to the base and those who manage to get closer than permitted are quickly removed by the guards watching the perimeter.

The exact location of Area 51 remains undisclosed, and cannot be found on most maps that are accessible to the public. Aviation maps and charts mark Area 51 as restricted airspace, and warn pilots that flying in the area is strictly prohibited. Some maps mark the area as "federal land", but exclude details of the existence of the base or any buildings located inside of it.

Despite most people knowing that this type of base must be closely watched and guarded at all times for obvious reasons, conspiracy theorists, as they are known to do, have come up with a number of alternate reasons for this secrecy, the majority of which revolve around extraterrestrial presence.

Alleged alien presence

Since the U.S. government hasn't been very forthcoming in regards to Area 51, on occasion even denying its existence completely, this added even more fuel to the fire and lit up the imaginations of those already open to the idea of an alien presence in our world.

On top of all the mystery and heavy military presence surrounding the area, there are also reports of mysterious lights appearing in the sky above Area 51. Of course, for those not buying into these conspiracy theories, it is not strange for these lights to appear over the military base known for testing new aircraft. But for the others, aliens are the only possible conclusion.

The number of people interested in what is going on behind the perimeter of the base is truly impressive. Guards on the outside rim usually have their hands full, dealing with the civilians who don't respect the boundaries and try to enter the protected zone. Although the guards are allowed to even use deadly force to protect the integrity of Area 51, this almost never happens. In most instances, intruders are escorted out and receive a fine around $600. After paying their fine, trespassers have a follow-up visit from the FBI, and anyone caught with photography or film cameras will have their equipment confiscated. I guess some would say that this is a small price to pay for the truth, so to each their own.

Recording videos or taking pictures inside the secure area is strictly forbidden though, and those found to doing so always have their recording equipment seized, and it is not unusual for the FBI agents to pay them a visit afterward. Some will take this as yet another clear indication that there is evidence of extraterrestrial life hidden inside Area 51, but the truth might be much more straightforward. This is a highly classified military operation, and the last thing they need are people running around with cameras, filming without any restrictions.

Main conspiracy theories

There are several conspiracy theories connected to Area 51. Most of them revolve around extraterrestrial presence, but there are some other quite interesting ideas. Some of the things that have been said about this base include the ideas that Area 51 is used to store and examine UFOs, to develop advanced weapons and technologies for weather control, time travel, teleportation, as well as stealth technologies. Some also believe that human - alien hybrids are being created inside of the base using the extraterrestrial samples from the area. It has even been speculated that Area 51 is used as a base for collaboration between humans and extraterrestrials. What they would be collaborating on can only be imagined. Other conspiracy theorists link Area 51 to the New World Order, saying the base is being used to create and organize a one-world government. Other, more plausible theories suggest the development of advanced camouflage technologies, or plans for an underground railroad that will run across the continent.

It is very likely that Area 51 is utilized to build and test aircrafts. One of the most highly regarded stealth aircrafts in existence, the Aurora Project, is said to fly around Area 51. The Aurora Project is thought to be fastest aircraft ever built, and can allegedly achieve speeds up to Mach 6.

Official statements on Area 51

Though very little information is available on Area 51, the government has made a handful of official statements regarding the base over the years. Presidential Determination No. 98-36, written by President Bill Clinton, exempts the "location Near Groom Lake, Nevada", or Area 51, from "any Federal, State, interstate, or local hazardous or solid waste laws that might require the disclosure of classified information concerning that operating location to unauthorized persons". The letter states that the disclosure of any information from Area 51 would be harmful to the nation's security.

An official response to questions about Area 51 from Mayor Jeffrey A. Rammes denied the existence of a base named "Area 51" but did confirm the operation of a base near Groom Dry Lake, Nevada. Rammes' response states that past and present activities being conducted at this base were to remain classified.

In November of 2011, the Obama administration released a statement meant to put extraterrestrial rumors to rest, but instead, sparked even more interest from conspiracy theorists. The statement read, "The U.S. government has no evidence that any life exists outside our planet, or that an extraterrestrial presence has contacted or engaged any member of the human race. In addition, there is no credible information to suggest that any evidence is being hidden from the public's eye". This was the first time in United States history that an executive branch took a formal stance on the existence of extraterrestrial life.

What to believe?

The majority of the world's population sees Area 51 for what it is: a highly classified, heavily guarded military base used to develop new technologies and weapons. One would not have to extend his imagination very far to come to a conclusion that there are probably some things happening inside that the government and the military would prefer to keep secret. But is this evidence or even an indication of the alien presence in the area?

It is only natural for human beings to create myths and legends around the places where access is restricted. This is even more so when such a place is known to deal with highly advanced technologies and is protected by armed guards with a license to kill if anyone tries to go beyond the limits.

All this indicates the existence of some dark, horrible secrets inside, but this isn't necessarily true. Every military secret is treated with special attention, and you wouldn't be allowed to roam freely through any military base on the planet. In the case of Area 51, it just happens that there are probably a large number of important secrets kept at the same base, requiring heavy supervision.

Whether you choose to believe in aliens or not is a matter of opinion. The universe is truly vast and trying to flat out deny the possibility of the existence of another intelligent life form is a bit short-sighted and quite close-minded. That said, it is very unlikely that the U.S. military keeps alien prisoners or remains of their starships hidden behind the fences of Area 51.

Chapter 7 – Roswell

Are we alone in the universe? Are there any other sentient beings from other planets besides earth? If there were, why haven't we heard from them yet? Conspiracy theorists believed that extraterrestrials have actually met humans, but the government is hiding them, and their technology in a secluded military base in the middle of the Nevada desert.

There were probably many times before when people have encountered extraterrestrials, but it was only when news reports from Roswell, New Mexico became public that UFOs and aliens became mainstream. The government has been trying its hardest to persuade the public that there was no evidence of alien activity in this once small, rural town.

How it all began

On June 14, 1947, while making his daily rounds of his ranch, Mac Brazel and his 8-year old son stumbled upon a strange wreckage. At first, Brazel thought nothing much about it, as he was already tired after a long day of work and he just wanted to go back home. However, the next morning, he heard over the news that people saw strange flying disks hovering over the town. Brazel thought that what he saw the day before may have been connected with the news reports. So he and his family went back to the crash site and recovered as much of the debris as they possibly could.

The amount of material they got was quite substantial, and they were also quite weird. There were large bits of shiny, elastic material, some stiff plastics, and some strong wood. Since he did not actually see the UFO crash, Brazel had no idea what the "craft" should look like.

The next morning, Brazel went to Roswell to sell some of the wool he got from the ranch. He figured that while he was in town, it would probably be wise to report his discovery to Roswell Sheriff George Wilcox, who then passed the message to Major Jesse Marcel of the Roswell Army Air Field. Marcel and an unnamed civilian went with Brazel back to his home where they tried their best to recreate whatever it was that the wreckage came from, but to no avail. They gave up trying to reconstruct the UFO and Maj. Marcel took the debris back to Roswell Air Field with him, and that was the last that Brazel ever saw of them again.

The following days, news broke out that the wreckage of an alien UFO was discovered in Roswell, and ever since then the media and alien enthusiasts have started flocking into this once unknown desert town.

Government cover-up

It was not really clear what it was that Brazel found in his ranch, but it was quite interesting that the US government suddenly went out and claimed it was the debris of a crashed weather balloon. It was even reported that the army might have harassed Mac Brazel into retracting his first statements and agreeing with the reports that what he saw might actually have been some kind of experimental weather balloon.

Even Major Marcel said that the debris was unlike anything he ever saw before, and this came from a man who had seen a multitude of airplanes and rockets in his long career. He was quite certain that they weren't parts of any aircraft he ever saw before.

Other evidence pointing to extraterrestrial involvement

Glen Dennis worked as a mortician in Roswell in the 1940's. Dennis claims that around the time of the crash, he was contacted by the military for several, small coffins. Dennis described feeling very strange when he arrived at the military base with the coffins, and even claims a nurse informed him that aliens had been recovered at the crash site.

Throughout Roswell's history, extraterrestrial beings have been physically described in multiple situations. Oddly enough, similar descriptions have been collected from numerous different sources. In almost all of the recorded accounts, the beings are described as being small and thin, with large, round eyes.

In the 1950s, suspicions of alien activity grew even further when a series of "dummy drops" were conducted over unoccupied fields in the New Mexico area. According to the United States Air Force, these "dummy drops" were experiments meant to test ways for pilots to survive falling from high altitudes. The problem was, the supposed "dummies" being dropped drew a striking resemblance to what was generally accepted as a space alien. The falling bodies were featureless with latex-like skin and aluminum-like bones. Upon a "dummy" landing, military vehicles were incredibly quick to retrieve them. Many believe these dummies were actually aliens being retrieved for experimentation by the government.

Since the crash in 1947, numerous UFO sightings and supernatural activity have been reported in Roswell and its surrounding areas. While it is possible these sightings were fueled by imagination, it is unlikely that all of the reports told of fictitious accounts.

Project Mogul

In an effort to dispel any doubts from the public, the US government "came clean" and announced that the parts recovered in Roswell, New Mexico came from an experimental, high-altitude surveillance balloon. The information released by the government stated that the balloon's purpose was to spy on the Soviets and warn the United States if ever it detected any nuclear threat.

According to the military, Project Mogul was a top-secret operation whose aim was to strap highly sensitive microphones on high-altitude weather balloons to detect any sound waves that Soviet nuclear bomb tests would have generated.

However, Brigadier General Thomas Dubose, who was present during the press conference that announced Project Mogul, later remarked that, "It was a cover story. The whole weather balloon part of it. That was the part of the story we were ordered to give to the public and the news." If that wasn't an admission of guilt then I don't know what is.

Even now, people are still flocking to Roswell in the hopes that they catch a glimpse of the alien wreckage, but it will never be seen again, as it was reportedly whisked off to the infamous Area 51 military base. Was there really an alien spacecraft that crash-landed in Roswell? Since the US government and the military is covering it up to the best of their abilities, odds are we will never find out.

Chapter 8 – The Bermuda Triangle

Even if you do not belong to the group of conspiracy theorists, you must have heard about the Bermuda Triangle or, as it is often called in popular culture, "The Devil's Triangle." This is a triangle-shaped part of the ocean enclosed by Bermuda on the North, Puerto Rico to the South, and Miami to the West.

There is nothing special about this location regarding its geographic characteristics; the odds are that most people would have never heard about it in the first place if it wasn't for the mysterious disappearances of ships and aircraft traveling through or over the Bermuda Triangle region.

According to maritime experts, there is nothing particularly dangerous about this area and there is no evidential reason for these disappearances. Not surprisingly, this only fueled the fire for strange thoughts, and people have developed some outlandish theories about the "Devil's Triangle." Some of them do have certain scientific explanations attached to them, while the others are just fruit from someone's imagination running wild.

Strange compass readings

Some of the last messages received from the vehicles that disappeared in the Bermuda Triangle were along the lines of "our compass is going crazy." Although it is always hard to determine what exactly was going on just before a disaster, it is clear from these messages that ships were not able to navigate properly, likely causing their demise.

This gave conspiracy theorists many ideas, the most prominent of which are those about the alien activity in this region and abductions of unwitting passengers. When one always looks for conspiracies and mysteries in everything, this explanation fits the bill nicely.

The science, however, has a different explanation. There are certain places on Earth where a compass goes haywire and doesn't point to the north. These places include the Gobi

Desert, North, and South Poles, and, you guessed it, the Bermuda Triangle. This anomaly could clearly be the cause for an extraordinary number of accidents and disappearances in the region, but there is most certainly nothing extraterrestrial about it.

Gulf Stream influence

If we blame incorrect compass readings for accidents, the question remains why so often there are no traces of these aircrafts and vessels to be found anywhere? It is one thing for a ship to sink but entirely different for it to go missing completely.

Once again this gives backing to alien theories, as it is "clear" that the reason why these ships and planes are rarely recovered is that aliens took them. The scientific explanation is, or at least one of them, is much more realistic and, as is usually the case, far less exciting.

The Gulf Stream is one of the major oceanic currents, extending from the Gulf of Mexico to the North Atlantic. Although a current by nature, it acts more like a river, achieving speeds of 2.5 meters per second (about 9 km per hour). Since the Gulf Stream passes through the Bermuda Triangle, it could easily pull any debris miles away from the original place of accident very quickly. By the time search and rescue parties get there, those unfortunate ships and planes can be long gone.

Deposits of methane hydrate

This is one of the more scientific and credible theories about the Bermuda Triangle disappearances. The research conducted in this area has confirmed that there are, in fact, large deposits of methane hydrate under the ocean beds on the continental shelves. Bubbles caused by the methane eruptions increase the water density and can cause ships to go under. When something like this happens, it is often so quick that affected vehicles don't even have time to send out an SOS message.

While the theory is somewhat plausible, many scientists argue that the Bermuda Triangle region is hardly the only site in the world where methane hydrate deposits are found. There are numerous places with similar properties, and there is no reason why the "Devil's Triangle" would be more dangerous than any of them. On top of that, there is no record of strong methane gas releases in the last 15,000 years.

Weather conditions

There is no doubt that the weather in this region is not the most favorable to travelers. With hurricanes, storms, and cyclones, these strange weather conditions can get ships and planes in trouble very quickly. Recorded weather changes have sometimes been so fast and powerful that they are likened to bomb explosions, easily powerful enough to bring down aircraft and sink ships.

Of all the theories, this one seems like the most likely to be true. Highly volatile weather conditions, coupled with the Gulf Stream, could easily account for disasters and disappearances of all sorts of vehicles in this region.

The time warp theory

Moving away from the real science, we once again step into the world of impossible and fantasy. One theory upheld by a number of conspiracy theorists is that of the time warp existing in the Bermuda Triangle region.

According to this theory, those missing planes and ships enter a rip in time-space continuum and travel through time, finding themselves at the same place but in a different period. This can be either past or future, but because of this dislocation, it is impossible to locate vehicles or any traces of them.

Some of them are unable to find the portal again and are thus stuck in whatever time they were teleported to. Others manage to find the way back, and this is why some of them are found after a while.

As for what happens to these vehicles on the "other side," we can only guess. The recovered ships are usually found in very bad condition, but whether this was caused by the travel itself or by something that happened after the journey into the triangle is anybody's guess.

The Atlantis theory

There are numerous tales, myths, and legends revolving around the lost city of Atlantis. According to writings that have come to light, this was a very advanced civilization, so far ahead of their contemporaries that even our modern civilization cannot compare to them. Plato asserts that this city flourished in 9600 BC and, if he is to be believed, Atlantis was a society unlike anything else the world has seen. However, a catastrophic disaster hit the city and wiped it off the face of the earth in a single day.

It is believed that Atlantis was hit by a disastrous flood that completely submerged the city, covering it with the sea and killing the entire population. To this day, its location remains a mystery; but not according to conspiracy theorists.

A large group of those looking to find answers to the mysterious Bermuda Triangle disappearances believe that the city was located somewhere in this area and that the radiation emanating from the submerged devices causes the electronic equipment on ships and planes to go crazy.

The theory was strengthened by the discovery of a human-made rock formation called Bimini Road. Those inclined to believe that Atlantis was submerged right in the middle of the "Devil's Triangle" hope that more discoveries will be made in the future, proving their theory. The problem is, the sea is so deep here that it is practically impossible for the scientists to come up with any conclusive or definite results.

Pirate attacks

Another not so ludicrous theory about the Bermuda Triangle disappearances is that of pirate attacks happening in the region. This part of the world has been known for frequent pirate attempts on all sorts of ships, especially during the peak years of disappearances. Pirates were known for their cruelty, and it was a part of their MO to sink the ships after they were done looting so they wouldn't have to deal with hostages or to hide the evidence.

This theory makes a lot of sense if we consider the period and the area where disappearances took place. The Bermuda Triangle was certainly a great hunting territory for these scoundrels, so it would be no surprise to find out that pirates were, in fact, behind some of these "mysterious" events.

Gravitation anomalies

The final theory we will consider regarding the "Devil's Triangle" is that of strange gravitational forces acting in the area. According to this theory, there is a mass concentration of gravitation pulls in the region. The existence of these so-called "mascons" is a scientific fact, although no one has been able to determine what actually causes them.

As for the Bermuda Triangle, it is quite possible for these "mascons" to exist in the area. Whether they are powerful enough to bring ships to the bottom is a different question altogether. While this is not a definite answer to the question of disappearances, it is something worth considering when discussing this topic.

It's all one big lie

Aside from all these theories, there is also a large group of people who are convinced that there is, in fact, no such a place as the Bermuda Triangle. It is all just a myth created by writers and filmmakers who came up with these popular stories and turned them into the hype.

These theorists believe that the number of vehicles disappearing in this part of the world is no greater than any other area where there is a lot of traffic. In fact, they claim, when compared to other maritime accidents around the globe, the events taking place in the Bermuda Triangle are hardly surprising or a statistical anomaly of any sort.

What to believe?

The Bermuda Triangle myth is probably one of the best-known stories of the 20th century. Mysterious accidents, disturbing SOS calls, and inexplicable disappearances have become a part of popular culture to such an extent that discerning the truth from fiction is nearly impossible.

All things considered, the "Devil's Triangle" represents a great territory for all those with excessive imaginations: conspiracy theorists and writers alike. But one must draw a line somewhere.

Saying that the Bermuda Triangle doesn't exist is probably going too far, but connecting it to some supernatural or extraterrestrial forces is equally so. Some of the scientific explanations are quite plausible, and there is little reason to go searching for the truth outside of them.

That said, it would be pretty cool if they ended up discovering the remains of Atlantis in the sea's depths one day.

Chapter 9 – 9/11 Terror Attack

You have probably heard about the 9/11 attack that brought down the twin towers of the World Trade Center and claimed thousands of lives. The media reported that this was a terrorist act perpetrated by the Al Qaeda, but what if I told you that there is more to the tragedy than what the news tells you? What would you do if you learned that it was all a ploy by the US government?

The motivation for the 9/11 attack

Conspiracy theorists believe that the reason for the WTC attack was the US government's greed. They believe that the government started to lose its position as the strongest country in the world, especially since up and coming economies like that of China were starting to gain ground. In order for the US to retain its lead over all of the other global superpowers, it needed access to additional finances, and the best way to get it is by peddling oil to developing countries. However, the US does not have enough oil in its reserves; it barely has enough of the stuff to fuel its own industries.

In order to get their hands on more oil, they needed to make an excuse to invade, or as they say, "increase their presence", in oil producing countries. This is why they devised a devious plan to stage a terrorist attack of such magnitude that the citizens of the world would not question their actions when they started attacking, and eventually taking over, oil-rich states.

"But, didn't two planes crash into the Twin Towers? Isn't that enough evidence of a terror attack?" is what most people ask when they first hear about 9/11 being an inside job. However, there are reasons to believe that it wasn't the planes that brought down the Twin Towers.

Theory 1 – Controlled demolition

Demolition expert Danny Jowenko believes that the reason why the WTC Towers collapsed was controlled explosions.

Upon closer inspection of the footage of the towers just before they collapsed, Jowenko said you will see a series of small explosions bursting out of the windows a couple of stories BELOW where the planes crashed.

There is also that famous cellphone video where you could hear popping noises from the first tower just before it imploded and crashed into the ground.

The most damning bit of evidence of controlled demolition was an eyewitness account from Marlene Cruz, a carpenter who was working in the World Trade Center during the "attack". In a television interview while she was in her hospital bed, she mentioned that there were explosions that came from the basement levels of the tower. Why would there be explosions in the basement of the tower when the plane crash-landed dozens of stories above it? Conspiracy theorists believe that the explosions came from explosives planted in the foundation of the building so that it would implode.

Theory 2 – Thermite use

Another theory that points to the controlled demolition job done of the World Trade Center towers comes from physicist Steven Jones. He pointed out that in one eyewitness video, there was a stream of white-hot glowing substance that came out of one of the towers. This evidence suggested that the final federal reports of molten aluminum being present could not be plausible, as melting aluminum would appear to be a silver-gray color in the daylight. Upon testing hardened bits of molten metal from the towers, Jones found they were not composed of structural steel, but mostly of iron. He said that these findings were evidence of an aluminothermic reaction, otherwise known as thermite use.

Thermite is a highly combustible mixture of powdered aluminum and iron oxide. When you set it on fire, nothing will stop it from burning until it completely oxidizes. Thermite can burn in high temperatures, often reaching thousands of degrees, which is clearly hot enough to melt metal as if it was nothing.

In 2002, a report written by Professor Jonathan Barnett noted evidence of sulfidation and oxidation. Sulfidation occurs when a small percentage of sulfur is added to Thermite in order to create a eutectic. This aids Thermite's steel-cutting properties, allowing it to do so more easily and at a lower temperature. Barnett stated in his report that, "No clear explanation for the source of the sulfur has been identified."

The official reports stated that the burning jet fuel and other combustible materials inside the towers weakened steel beams that supported the weight of the buildings. With the beams and posts compromised, it was only a matter of time before the towers collapsed. However, Steven Jones, and other 9/11 conspiracy theorists refute this claim; they believe that jet fuel and other materials that may have been in the towers that day would not have burned hot enough to compromise the buildings' structure.

Theory 3 – The planes were not hijacked

In the event of plane hijackings, NORAD would have been alerted and they would have sent fighter jets to debilitate or shoot down the planes. However, on 9/11, you can observe a conspicuous lack of fighter jets attempting to intercept the hijacked flights.

Theory 4 – Inside traders in Wall Street knew about the attack beforehand

In the days before the 9/11 attacks, market analysts discovered that there was an unusual spike in the number of options placed against United Airlines, which was coincidentally the airline whose planes were hijacked by terrorists. Conspiracy theorists believe that Jewish firms were the ones that tipped off the traders into selling UA stocks because they knew they would start plummeting in the next couple of days.

Theory 5 – The "plane" that crashed into the pentagon

Perhaps in an attempt to make the attacks seem more realistic, the powers-that-be behind the 9/11 attacks decided it would make sense if one of the hijacked planes were to crash into the Pentagon, which is the bastion of US defense. However, they might have left out a couple of important details.

For one thing, the hole left by the "airliner" that crashed into the Pentagon was quite small, especially since a commercial jet supposedly made it. The hole left by the hijacked plane was roughly 70 feet across, much too small for an airliner.

Another convenient little coincidence is that the plane fortunately crashed into a closed off part of the Pentagon that was scheduled for maintenance work. In other words, the plane crashed into an unoccupied part of the building, the odds of that happening by accident is downright miniscule.

Theory 6 – The phone calls made by the passengers were fake

Conspiracy theorists believe that the cellphone calls made by some of the passengers to their loved ones were fake, and that they were only used to gain sympathy from the public and get them outraged at the "terrorists".

One of the reasons why conspiracy theorists believe the phone calls were fake was because commercial airliners fly at altitudes that are too high for cellular towers to reach. In other words, there should not have been any cellphone reception while the planes were still in the air.

One passenger from one of the flights called his mother before he and the other passengers tried to fight the hijackers. The strange thing about the call was he referred to himself using his full name. Who does that kind of thing when talking to their own mother?

Theory 7 – A disturbingly huge number of Jewish workers took the day off

Conspiracy theorists found out that more than 4,000 Jewish workers in the World Trade Center took the day off on

9/11/01. This was quite unusual, especially since there were no Jewish holidays that fell on that day. Another reason why conspiracy theorists are wary of the Jews is that most of the eyewitness camera footage came from people of Jewish descent; it's as if they knew they had to pull out their cellphone cameras at just the right time.

It was rumored by Arab diplomatic sources that World Trade Center workers of Jewish decent were tipped off by the Israeli General Security apparatus, the Shabak. American officials quickly became suspicious upon hearing the reports, but the question was, why would Israel perpetrate an attack on its strongest ally? Conspiracy theorists believe that in staging the attack, America would have no choice but to turn against Muslim countries once and for all. Conspiracists believe Israel's motivation to carry out the attack was to force its strongest ally to aid them in fighting their worst enemy, Palestine.

These are just some of the conspiracy theories that surround one of the most publicized disasters in history. It may seem callous of conspiracy theorists to throw shade on the people who died on that day, but if you just keep an open mind about what they said, you just cannot help but think that there might be something to their arguments.

Chapter 10 – The War on Terror

If there is one thing that marked the second half of the 20th century, it's the notion of terrorism and the "war on terror," waged primarily by the United States and their European allies. There is no denying that certain events that took place during the past twenty or thirty years call for stern and determined actions, but who is really behind it all?

One of the biggest conspiracy theories of the modern era revolves around the notion that the entire concept of the "war on terror" is a pure fabrication, made up by the world powers to give them free reign to do what they want and expand their global influence. Particular documents and testimonies do seem to back up these claims at least to an extent, so one must wonder, what is the truth?

Al Qaeda and the fight for oil

It is no secret that a bulk of the U.S. economy revolves around oil. It is also no secret that the majority of natural oil sources are located in the countries controlled by the Muslim majority. When George Bush Jr. took his seat in the oval office, there was already a plan in place for building a big oil pipeline through Afghanistan. This was a project of great value and not one that the U.S. government would allow to fall through under any circumstances. However, Taliban forces created a disturbance in these plans, and they had to be dealt with.

Osama Bin Laden came to prominence while fighting as a Mujahedeen soldier in Afghanistan. This group was fighting Soviets in the country and was backed by the U.S. government. Once the Soviets withdrew, the American support was gone, and the country was left on its own, thrown into the midst of a civil war.

According to conspiracy theorists, Bin Laden was funded by Saudi Arabia, under U.S. pressure, for his role as the leader of Al Qaeda. After the war with the Soviets was over, Bin Laden's idea of the Jihad started spreading all over the Middle East.

However, in 1996 things start to take a different turn. Bin Laden issued a fatwa against American forces in Saudi Arabia, Mecca, and Medina. In 1998, he returned to Afghanistan, and issued another fatwa, this time calling for a full-scale attack against American forces everywhere in the world.

During Clinton's time in the office, the U.S. response was restrained and limited to known Taliban military targets. The goal of these attacks was to pressure Afghan forces into handing over Osama Bin Laden who, by this point, has become their hero.

In 2001, with the arrival of George Bush Jr., everything would change. The September 11 attacks, described in the previous chapter, gave Americans the very reason they needed to win over the public opinion, and this started the war in Afghanistan.

Returning to the Unocal pipeline, it was practically impossible to put into action a plan this big with the Taliban in power in Afghanistan. Something had to be done, and quickly.

Whatever one chooses to believe about 9/11, it is quite clear that Americans had an ulterior motive for war with Afghanistan. The oil, which remains one of the most valuable resources of the modern era, is simply too important. The USA could not allow for this small faction to put a halt to their carefully crafted plans.

On top of this, the 9/11 attack gave an excuse to start what would become known as the global "war on terrorism." This idea about evil terrorists lurking in the shadows and waiting to strike put fear in the U.S. people, and gave the President a blank check to start military campaigns against other evil nations, like Iraq, North Korea, or Iran.

Not surprisingly, Iraq and Iran have the biggest oil reserves in the world. As soon as President Bush was done with Afghanistan, he turned his attention to Iraq, claiming Saddam had connections to Osama Bin Laden and 9/11 events. Neocon Zalmay Khalilzad, the U.S. ambassador to Afghanistan, was aptly moved to Iraq to smooth the transition.

Since we've already discussed possible conspiracies behind the September 11 events, we will not be coming back to those. Suffice to say, regardless of whether it was all one big conspiracy or 9/11 was, in fact, a terrorist attack, it gave the USA what they wanted. The attack gave them a reason to first invade Afghanistan and then declare the global war on terrorism, aptly tailored in such a manner to target oil-rich countries in the Middle East.

Bank of Credit and Commerce International

Osama bin Laden, Saddam Hussein, and President George W. Bush are all said to be linked by one common party, the BCCI, or Bank of Credit and Commerce International. Founded by Agha Hasan Abedi in 1972, the Bank of Credit and Commerce International was supposedly utilized by the Reagan administration for running guns to Saddam Hussein, financing Osama bin Laden, and moving money in the Iran-Contra operation. One of the BCCI's most affluent investors was reportedly responsible for bailing George W. Bush out of tanking oil investments.

The CIA used BCCI Islamabad and other branches in Pakistan to funnel upwards of two billion dollars to Osama bin Laden's Mujahadeen in order for him to help fight the Soviets in Afghanistan. Throughout the years, the United States funneled outrageous amounts of money through the BCCI, and after 20 years in business, the scandal became the biggest bank fraud in history. Upon further investigation of the Bush family and their ties to BCCI, it seems likely that President George W. Bush had close, financial connections to al Qaeda throughout the War on Terror.

The Islamic State (ISIS)

If you've been following the media during the recent years, you've probably come to realize that Al Qaeda is barely ever mentioned these days. It seems that this powerful terrorist organization has just vanished into thin air. However, there is another grave threat; that of the Islamic State or ISIS, as it is better known.

ISIS is the new enemy of the United States, and American armed forces, led by President Barack Obama, are doing everything in their power to stop them from their evil plans. However, many believe that ISIS is, in fact, a U.S. creation.

The most vehement supporters of this theory come from Iran, another country that the USA has had its eyes on for some time now. These Iranians believe that powerful figures in the American economy and politics have invented this group to help further their plans to destroy the Iranian capital, Teheran.

While Iranians may have very apparent reasons to believe that Americans are behind this conspiracy, they are not the only ones. An American newspaper, "The Final Call," has voiced their opinion that the U.S. and countries like Saudi Arabia and Turkey have been funding ISIS and helping them with training soldiers since 2007.

Of course, there are also somewhat more moderate conspiracy theories regarding ISIS. According to these, the Islamic State was not directly created by the USA, but they did allow for its rise to power through their invasion of Iraq.

Another theory about how ISIS came to be is that it was created by Israel and Jews to destroy Islam. According to this theory, ISIS is in fact led by a Mossad agent and the idea behind the movement is attacking countries that threaten Israel to help the country extend its political power and expand its territories.

What to believe?

The biggest problem when it comes to figuring out the high politics as an ordinary person is that it is almost impossible to do. We are simply not privy to enough information to make a reasonable conclusion, and the information we do have is often twisted or colored in such a way to propagate someone's political or other agenda.

The United States of America have certainly demonstrated their willingness and resolve to get involved in all sorts of conflicts where their interests might be at risk. That fact, combined with the knowledge that throughout history propaganda has been used to start wars and shift the public opinion make some of these conspiracy theories a real possibility.

There is little doubt that oil is one of the biggest interests in today's world, and having a world super power start a war or two over a significant amount of this resource would hardly be shocking. After all, throughout history wars were waged to obtain resources and not rarely under false pretenses. I don't think that much has changed in that regard.

Chapter 11 – Vaccines Are Bad

One of the conspiracy theories from the most recent period concerns vaccines and their effect on overall human health. Ever since the concept of the vaccine has been introduced, it helped save countless lives and, we can freely say that it really gave the human race a lot of room to advance without being in constant fear of dying from relatively harmless diseases.

But, if you ask conspiracy theorists, this is not so. Vaccines are the evil plan of modern medicine designed to actually ruin our lives. Everything we know and we've been told about vaccines is a lie, and there is no real reason for vaccination.

Vaccines causing autism

Before 1999, the vaccines contained the preservative known as thimerosal. This preservative was claimed to cause autism in children, and although there was no scientific proof to really back this claim, it was either completely removed or severely reduced in all vaccines for children. The only exception to this was the influenza vaccine, but as of late, these are also being prepared using only the very minimum of thimerosal.

The reason why thimerosal was brought in question in the first place was that it caused potentially high levels of mercury in children. Even though that only a few vaccines were made with thimerosal in the first place, there were numerous initiatives to do something about this issue.

However, it did not stop at this. The voices became louder, claiming that different preservatives and additives found in vaccines were harmful and could cause some serious damage to our health. These people refused the very basic scientific premise that these additives were simply necessary for a vaccine to do what is supposed to do. They are needed to keep the viruses and bacteria alive while at the same time weakening them enough so they cannot replicate and cause the full-fledged disease.

Basing beliefs on false information

The anti-vaccination propaganda grew stronger over the years, garnering the support of those who did not know what to believe. The claims that were being made by certain "authoritative" figures made sense. They were talking about poisonous elements inside the vaccines, like aluminum. Since thimerosal was removed, the aluminum had become new enemy number one.

The aluminum is, in fact, poisonous, but so are pretty much all the elements. What anti-vaccination propagators forget to mention is that the amount is of crucial important here. The aluminum is present only in small amounts in the vaccines, and it helps them produce a better immune response.

While the aluminum may be poisonous in excessive amounts, the amounts contained in the vaccines are far below any dangerous level. It was not introduced as a substitute for thimerosal at all, as it has a completely different purpose and it has been a part of the vaccines for a long time.

This did not prevent conspiracy theorists from propagating their myth about the correlation between vaccines and autism. They just shifted their focus to aluminum and continued telling the same story to anyone willing to listen. Proper scientific studies have proven that vaccines do not represent any serious threats for children and that the aluminum intake from the all suggested vaccines during the first year of life is very low.

Anti-vaccination myths

It is only natural for parents to be concerned for their children. However, when it comes to health related issues, unless they have medical training themselves, they are usually best off letting professionals do their business. However, the Internet and easy access to all sorts of information have created an environment where conspiracy theorists can easily share their opinions, and very often people are caught between two fires, not knowing whom to believe.

The anti-vaccination movement has started numerous myths that lead parents to believe that they can safely skip vaccinations without any consequences, or that they are doing more good than harm if they decide against vaccination. Apart from the widespread autism theory, there is a significant number of others that these conspiracy theorists spread using different media outlets.

People who get sick during outbreaks are usually vaccinated

This is absolutely not true. Looking at the percentages, most people who get sick during outbreaks are, in fact, not vaccinated. This is just another myth propagated by those trying to deny the health benefits of vaccines. Numbers to confirm this theory are usually twisted in such a way as to dwarf the truth. For example, if there are 1,000 kids in school, 900 of them vaccinated and 100 of them not, and there is an outbreak, statistically speaking, the percentage of unvaccinated children who get ill will be much higher. E.g., if 50 kids get mumps, 28 of them vaccinated and 22 not, then it is clear that a much higher percentage of those unvaccinated students actually got ill.

Diseases that vaccines prevent are not really that serious

Yet another theory that doesn't hold water. Prior to vaccines, a great number of people died of these not-so-serious diseases all over the world. The reason why this theory even flies is because these times are long behind us, and we do not remember the devastating effects some of these diseases had on the world's population.

Vaccines successfully stopped epidemics and had pretty much prevented any big outbreaks, but looking at some numbers before the vaccinations tells a different story. Polio caused between 13,000 and 20,000 cases of paralytic poliomyelitis every year in the USA. Measles took between 500 and 1,000 lives on a yearly basis, and there were around half a million of cases every year. Diphtheria killed 15,000 every year.

Most people do not vaccinate their kids

This is just something that people tell themselves to feel better about their decision and it is, of course, propagated by the anti-vaccination movement. However, this is far from being factual.

The vast majority of people decide to vaccinate their children during their early childhood to protect them from the common diseases. A 2012 CDC report confirmed that between 90% and 95% of children have received most of their vaccines by the age of 3.

If it seems to you like you know many parents who decide not to vaccinate, it is probably because they tend to cluster together and are very vocal about their beliefs. People who do vaccinate do not talk about it as much. The vaccination has become commonplace in the modern society and most people just take it for granted.

Vaccines are made using aborted fetal tissue

This statement has a clear purpose of winning over those who are against abortion and creating very unpleasant imagery even in the heads of those who are not against vaccinations. But, once again, this is a complete lie.

There were only two very particular occasions in the 1960s when tissue was created to grow the viruses needed for the vaccine, and one of these was the rubella vaccine. The vaccine helped stop a horrible epidemic in 1964 which caused thousands of deaths and spontaneous abortions. It was the only possible solution to a big problem.

It is important to note that even in this case, no one actually performed an abortion to provide the tissue for the vaccine. The tissue of aborted fetuses was simply used for a good cause.

But back to the main topic, these were exceptions rather than rules. Vaccines are generally not made using aborted fetal tissue, regardless of what anti-vaccination propaganda is trying to tell you.

Natural immunity is sufficient and better than vaccines

No one denies that natural immunity in humans is a great thing. In fact, vaccines are based on this very concept and help you develop the natural immunity at a much faster pace.

If you want your children to develop this immunity without vaccines, then they will have to actually suffer through the full-fledged diseases, which can last for days or even weeks and consequences can often be hard to predict. Do not be fooled by propaganda and conspiracy theories, some of these diseases can have life-threatening implications or cause long-term damage.

On top of this, natural immunity can be very volatile. Vaccines are designed and tested to produce the best possible results in the great majority of people. With natural immunity, things can go either way, and you may end up suffering from a disease only to catch it again a few years later.

Quarantine is the solution

One of the anti-vaccination propaganda points is that sick people should simply stay home, and this would severely reduce the possibility of an outbreak. This is a nice notion but even if all parents were so observing and responsible, there is another problem.

In most childhood infections, children become infectious before the first symptoms appear. This means that one child could infect their entire class without even realizing they are sick. With many of these infections, you could carry the infection around for a few days prior to realizing that it is in your system, and by that point, it is usually too late for quarantine.

Vaccines are against most religions

When everything else fails, there is always religion. Sticking to religion has worked throughout the ages to justify even the wildest, most bizarre arguments. It often works because people are not that well acquainted with all the rules of their religion and are willing to take someone else's word for it.

The fact is that there are only a few small religious factions that are completely opposed to vaccination, like Christian Scientists. But, the religious objection, combined with an irrational fear, is often enough to keep people from getting their vaccines.

Many medical experts are against vaccines

This is completely false. The majority of medical experts fully support vaccines and recognize them for what they are. Very few people within the medical field are openly against vaccines, and those who are usually aren't experts in the field.

Once again, these people are very vocal about their opinions so it may seem that there are more of them than there really are. Don't be fooled into thinking that the medical community is somehow divided on the vaccination issue just because a small faction has a different view.

Vaccines are used without proper testing

Another bogus theory about vaccines is that they are not properly tested or that they are not tested together for possible reactions. Vaccines are, in fact, tested together to see the results and avoid any complications as much as possible.

Even after the vaccine is deemed safe, it is still constantly monitored for problems that could arise from unexpected circumstances, and as soon as something like this happens, new tests and safety measures are implemented.

Of course, there is a possibility of adverse reaction in some cases, but this is true for pretty much all medicines and medical treatments. Using this as a reason to avoid vaccination is nothing but propaganda.

It is safer to vaccinate your kids when they grow older

This is most certainly not true. Infants and toddlers have the biggest risk of contracting childhood diseases. If they happen to get infected, possible complications represent the biggest threat while they are still very young, and their immune systems are not adequately developed.

The idea behind this belief is that older children will be less susceptible to vaccination side-effects. This is not true, either, so you will basically just be leaving your child unprotected for a longer period of time for no good reason.

What to believe?

Based on the tone and opinions shared throughout this chapter, it is probably quite clear what you should believe. Vaccination is not a bad thing, it will not put your child at grave risk, and they will not be poisoned by different harmful elements and chemicals.

In fact, the discovery of vaccines is probably one of the best things that ever happened to humankind in its entire history. It helped prevent epidemics which previously took the lives of children and grownups alike year after year, all over the world.

Are there risks connected to vaccination? Yes, of course there are. There are risks connected to almost any remotely serious decision you make in your life. But the risks of skipping vaccination altogether are much more serious and have much more dangerous implications.

By deciding against vaccination, or delaying it without a legitimate reason, you will be putting your child at risk, and possibly exposing them to serious complications that childhood infections can cause. Do not be fooled by propaganda and seemingly innocuous common names for these infections. They can be very serious.

Chapter 12 – Chemtrails

Anyone who has looked up at the sky in recent years is sure to have noticed white streaks trailing across the horizon at some point. While most people write off these white lines as vapor or the after-effects of passing planes, many conspiracists have a different theory... chemtrails.

The purpose of chemtrails

In recent years there has been much suspicion surrounding these white trails that can often be spotted in the sky. The general consensus among conspiracy theorists is that these seemingly harmless white lines are actually chemical filled pollutants. While there is no doubt the air is being polluted by factories, cars, and other day to day occurrences, theorists believe these white trails, referred to as chemtrails, are packed with particular toxins including aluminum, barium, lead, arsenic, chromium, cadmium, selenium, and silver. These harmful pollutants are linked to a flurry of health problems ranging from neurological effects, heart damage, eyesight issues, and reproductive failures to immune system damage, gastrointestinal disorders, damaged kidneys, damaged livers, hormonal problems, and more.

Evidence of the existence of chemtrails

Conspiracists believe the government is deliberately filling the air with these poisons in order to reduce the size of the population, and to perform biological tests on the masses. Chemtrails are also said to be utilized in matters of geoengineering and weather modification. The most reputable proof of this phenomenon comes from a 2007 video of Dr. Rosalind Peterson, the president of California's Agriculture Defense Coalition. The video takes place at Climate Change conference organized by the United Nations. In her speech, Dr. Peterson addresses the use of airborne chemicals in order to manipulate changes in the climate. Peterson states that the chemicals in question accelerate the effects of global warming and create "man-made clouds" in the sky.

The 2009 History Channel series, *That's Impossible*, revealed the existence of many technologies that seem to be pulled straight from science fiction. In one episode entitled, "Weather Warfare," evidence was presented that US Military had mechanisms available to them that could manipulate massive, strategic weather changes. While weather modification sounds wildly outlandish, its existence could be detrimental. In 2009, China admitted to using weather modification to clear smog from the air prior to a parade celebrating the 60th anniversary of Communist China. A Chinese meteorologist explained that a chemical was dispersed into the air in order to cause a light rain that would clear the smog. He also stated that another different chemical was on-hand in order to stop the rain if it were to continue for too long. Russia also admitted to the use of weather modification chemicals in 2009, when the mayor of Moscow promised to keep snow out of the city. He achieved this by employing the Russian Air Force to spray chemicals into the clouds before they could reach the capital city. This made it so the clouds would release the snow outside of the city instead.

What conspiracy theorists believe are chemtrails are often referred to as "contrails", short for "condensation trails", by government officials. While contrails are what is typically left behind from passing jets, chemtrails are said to differ in appearance. In November 2007, a segment aired on Louisiana's KSLA News channel covering the story of a man who claimed to spot this difference. Upon noticing the peculiar lines in the sky, the man also began noticing small particles falling from the sky. The man collected these particles in a small bowl, and gave the samples to KSLA News for testing. When the lab results came back, the particles were found to contain high levels of Barium, a highly toxic substance, along with other strange chemicals. In fact, the Barium levels found in the samples were many times over what the EPA classifies as toxic.

In October 2001, the Space Preservation Act of 2001 (H.R. 2977) was introduced by Congressmen Dennis Kucinich. In the bill, chemtrails are mentioned as an exotic weapon. The bill states its purpose is to "preserve the cooperative, peaceful uses of space for the benefit of all humankind by permanently prohibiting the basing of weapons in space by the United States, and to require the President to take action and implement a world treaty banning space-based weapons".

The 1977 release of documents titled "US Army Activity in the US Biological Warfare Programs" revealed the deliberate use of biological agents in 239 populated areas between the years of 1949 and 1969. The unclassified pages explain that areas were contaminated by the US Army for the purpose of secret testing. One test described in the documents utilized scientists in disguises spraying bacteria in Ronald Reagan Washington National Airport. Another detailed a jet releasing material over Victoria, TX. The same document annotates a Navy ship that sprayed material into the San Francisco Bay over a 30-mile span, while other similar tests involved spraying like materials into the New York City subway system. These tests were said to have affected people with weakened immune systems.

Evidence of the non-existence of chemtrails

Though it may not be easy to ignore the evidence that chemtrails exist, there are many arguments against their existence as well. The main argument against chemtrails is that these white lines in the sky are simply the condensation from aircrafts, or contrails, as mentioned before. The surge in the appearance of these trails is explained by an upsurge in aircraft usage and air travel in recent years. The cirrus, or spreading of these contrails is explained by high levels of humidity in the air, and a lack of wind keeping the condensation from dissipating. Some argue that the use of chemtrails to make the populace sick would backfire on those perpetuating their use, as we are all breathing the same air, but these simple explanations do not satisfy those who firmly believe in the existence of chemtrails.

What to believe?

There is valid evidence supporting both the existence and non-existence of chemtrails, so it is difficult to know what to believe. As of now, the only irrefutable method of weather modification is cloud seeding, which uses aircraft to sprinkle clouds with silver iodine, or dry ice, in an attempt to change the amount or type of rain that falls from clouds. This method is typically utilized to lessen the effects of hurricanes, but it is definitely not fail-safe.

If the government truly had an agenda to keep its population sick, there is no doubt they would try hard to keep it under wraps, but it is very hard to say whether or not this phenomenon is legitimate, or simply imagined by paranoid minds.

Chapter 13 – FBI "False Flags"

The Federal Bureau of Investigation is the United States' first and last line of defense against domestic and foreign threats, and they do almost anything imaginable (sometimes unimaginable) so they can do their jobs. There are many cases when the FBI had to resort to using "false flags" to garner public approval for something that they would otherwise protest.

A "false flag" is a covert operation wherein the people involved make it look like it was other groups that did it, in other words, it's a cover-up. The FBI, whether they admit to it or not, is no stranger to doing cover-up and false flag operations, and conspiracy theorists have been digging up a lot of their previous clandestine missions, and some of them were really sinister in nature.

"False flag" operations are not used only to hide the real perpetrators but they also often serve as a frame-up, shifting the blame to another party to achieve a certain political or military agenda. As such, it is no wonder why they attract the attention of different groups and individuals trying to uncover conspiracies.

The problem with these operations is that they are covert by nature, meaning there is very little, if any evidence, and whatever does get uncovered must be taken with a big pinch of salt, as it is sometimes impossible to determine what is the real evidence and what was purposely left to be uncovered.

COINTELPRO

COINTELPRO was a series of false flag operations orchestrated by the FBI that targeted socio-political groups from the 50s all the way to the 70s. The purpose of COINTELPRO is to discredit the many political activist groups to prevent them from gaining more traction. Some of their most targeted groups include that of Dr. Martin Luther King, and the groups that protested the involvement of the US in the Vietnam War.

The way the FBI carried out these operations was thru planting their own people inside these groups, and then making them commit various crimes that would smear the group's name. Other methods the FBI used for this false flag operation included, but are not limited to, leaking forged documents and reports to the media, wrongful imprisonment, and there was also quite a lot of speculation about the involvement of violence and assassinations.

Conspiracy theorists believe that COINTELPRO is still in effect today, citing that they were recently active in preventing the Occupy Wall Street movement from growing.

The Iraq war

Probably one of the most popular, which also means it's the worst kept secret of the FBI, is when the US pinned the 9/11 attacks on the Iraqi government. Even after the 9/11 Commission fessed up that there was no connection between Al Qaeda and the Saddam Hussein-led Iraq, then Vice President Dick Cheney was adamant that there was sufficient evidence for going through with the declaration of war.

The truth is, according to conspiracy theorists, the war was not for retaliation, but for the US to gain a foothold in one of the world's leading suppliers of oil.

The Oklahoma City bombing

On April 19, 1995, when Timothy McVeigh drove a truck laden with explosives into the Federal Building in downtown Oklahoma City, the media immediately concluded that it was a "lone wolf" attack of a crazed military radical. The resulting blast, which killed almost 200 people and injured 700, was one of the most devastating domestic act of violence that hit the US. However, according to conspiracy theorists, there was more to the event than what the media wanted people to know.

According to conspiracy theorists, Timothy McVeigh was a pawn pre-programmed by the FBI. The purpose of the entire operation was to cull the growing number of militia groups in the US, which started growing at a surprisingly fast rate after the Waco Massacre. One of the reasons why conspiracy theorists refuse to believe the version of the story mentioned in the media is that explosive experts had already come forward, and claimed that fertilizer bombs should not have been strong enough to blow off an entire face of a reinforced concrete building.

The FBI has always said that they always have the country's best interest in mind when they do covert operations, but you seriously have to doubt them when they start sacrificing the lives of thousands of people just to get results. The end does not justify the means.

The Sandy Hook Elementary School shooting

The Sandy Hook Elementary School shooting was an extremely controversial matter, as it involved the deaths of 20 grade school children, as well as 6 adults. On December 14th, 2012 in Newton, CT, tragedy struck when 20-year-old Adam Lanza took three guns, one being a semi-automatic AR-15 assault rifle, into Sandy Hook Elementary School and began firing. After the incident, Lanza took his own life. Investigators later found that he also killed his mother prior to going to the school.

When the event was further researched by conspiracy theorists, the Sandy Hook Elementary School shooting seemed to have countless inconsistencies. Former law enforcement officer and Sandy Hook researcher, Wolfgang Halbig discovered thirteen different Sandy Hook memorial websites created before the event ever took place. Halbig also found that the Sandy Hook Elementary website had absolutely no internet activity for four years prior to the event, raising suspicion that the school was not even active prior to the shooting. Halbig discovered evidence that 16 state troopers were pre-positioned near Sandy Hook 45 minutes to an hour before the shooting took place. In addition, a video taken inside the fire station up the street from the school, where children were told to flee to shows people entering the building through one door, circling the building then reentering through another door. This was likely to create the illusion of activity as well as more people.

Multiple sources state there is no record of the Sandy Hook Elementary School shooting in the FBI's 2012 crime report, and that there are no recorded social security numbers for any of the deceased. It is also said that crisis actors were employed to appear at the scene of the shooting, as well as give false reports to the media.

The Boston Marathon bombing

On April 15, 2013 two bombs detonated near the finish line of the celebrated Boston Marathon. The bombing resulted in the deaths of 3 onlookers, and wounded over 260 civilians. The attacks were said to have been carried out by 19-year-old, Dzhokhar Tsarnaev and his older brother, Tamerlan Tsarnaev, who was later killed in a shootout with law enforcement. Despite the suspect's capture, the incident was immediately met with suspicions from conspiracy theorists and the general public.

There was no shortage of evidence discovered by conspiracy theorists that pointed to signs of FBI involvement. Warnings about the bombing were discovered online before the event ever took place, making it apparent that some outsiders had knowledge of the plan. Though only 2 suspects were portrayed by the media, photos of four men wearing the same backpacks that were used to hide the bombs were discovered by theorists, with one man being identified as a hired military mercenary.

A photo of Tamerlan Tsarnaev taken at 1:53am on the morning of his death shows him "in custody" with his hands outstretched, awaiting to be handcuffed by the authorities. In the photo, Tsarnaev appears to be unwounded, with his clothing intact. Three hours later he was reported as deceased from blast and gunshot wounds. At what point did this happen if he was in police custody only hours prior?

Media coverage of the tragedy showed photos of spectators that many conspiracy theorists recognized from media coverage of previous tragedies such as the Sandy Hook shooting. Conspiracy theorists believe the motivation behind the Boston Marathon bombing was meant to distract the masses as the government passed CISPA, the Cyber Intelligence Sharing and Protection Act. The bill, while essentially portrayed as a cybersecurity bill, gives the FBI access to just about any personal information on any US citizen's computer network without requiring a search warrant.

Chapter 14 – False Flag Hitler

During the early 1930's, the Nazi party was gaining momentum in Germany. In 1933, they were finally inches away from their goal, as the general elections were near and the party had nearly ensured the necessary support to give them enough seats in the Parliament to make them the majority. If they could achieve this, they could then give their leader, Adolf Hitler, limitless power in the country.

The victory, however, was not a certainty. There were other parties with popular support that could steal the majority and foil their plans. To prevent this from happening, many believe the Nazi party proceeded to perform a false flag that would forever change the course of history.

The Reichstag fire

With just a few weeks remaining until the elections, the German Parliament, Reichstag, was set on fire. From the ferocity of the fire, it was apparent that this was not an accident. The Reichstag fire was clearly arson, but the real question was: who did it?

The Nazi party leader, Adolf Hitler, was quick to blame the Communists. They represented a serious threat to their plans and had to be dealt with somehow. A direct attack would not work as it would not garner the public support. Implicating the Communists in something like this, however, was perfect. The arson was deemed an act of terror and those guilty were certain to face a harsh punishment.

Setting the stage for Nazi Germany

In the weeks leading to the fire, Nazis had already instilled the fear of Communists in people through the organized violence on the streets. With the foundations laid out, they proceeded to the finishing strike.

Hermann Goering made a public proclamation stating he had the evidence to prove the Communists were behind the arson. With everything that had been happening, the Nazis managed to convince the President to sign the so-called Reichstag Decree.

This Decree used the fear of terrorism as an excuse to abolish all the freedom in Germany. With it, the Weimar Constitution had become obsolete. An individual no longer had the right to demand to know why he was being imprisoned, the freedom of the press was gone, and big public gatherings were prohibited.

All of this was enough to convince the general population that they had to give their support to the Nazi party. After all, they had their safety and welfare in mind, and they were battling the evil Communists.

Once they came into power, it did not take long for Nazis to start implementing the policy they had previously dreamed up. The Enabling Act was passed, allowing Hitler to enact legislations with the help of his advisors, not requiring consent from the Parliament. With this Act, the dictatorship was fully established; as one man was allowed to singlehandedly tailor the destiny of an entire nation.

Was the Reichstag fire a false flag?

Just like with all other conspiracies, it remains unclear to this day who was really to blame for the Reichstag fire. Did the Communists actually do it or did Nazis plan it all in order to discredit their biggest rivals? Or, perhaps, it was all an accident or act of an individual that Hitler and Goering took advantage of?

The only thing that was established as a fact and is agreed on by most historians is that Marinus van der Lubbe, a former Communist, and a mentally disturbed person, was found inside the Reichstag. Ironically enough, after the Nazis seized control, the Communists were actually found not guilty by the very Nazi government that used the accusations to ascend to power.

Those supporting the conspiracy theory, including a number of respected historians, share the conviction that Nazis in fact used van der Lube to commit the crime they needed done.

They did not only enable him to enter the building, but also encouraged him to set the place on fire.

Looking at the aftermath, it is hard to think anything else, but that Nazis orchestrated the whole thing and put in motion a really devious plan that would give them firm and complete control over the country and its citizens.

An alternate theory

If there is one common denominator for all conspiracy theories, then it's that not everybody shares the same opinion. Regarding the Reichstag fire, there are those who do not believe it was a false flag and are, in fact, convinced that the Communists did do it, and they also tried to blame it on Nazis.

The theory is not that ludicrous, of course, since if it was true the Nazis would have a hard time convincing the people of Germany in the first place. It was no secret that there was no love lost between Hitler and the Communist party. Those not believing that Nazis orchestrated the arson are convinced that it was an event designed to create a civil war in Germany and give power to the Communists.

What to believe?

There has never been overwhelming physical evidence about the Reichstag fire. This is hardly surprising considering everything went up in flames and, if it was a false flag, those behind it got exactly what they wanted.

While most conspiracies are not really clear cut, what happened in Germany in 1933 was highly likely the work of the Nazi party, as they ended up profiting the most from the event and its aftermath.

Chapter 15 – Hitler in Argentina

Continuing on the topic of historical events, we will now deal with another widespread conspiracy theory regarding Adolf Hitler's suicide. The official history claims that the Nazi Germany leader took his own life on April 30, 1945, as the allied forces were making their way through Berlin. Hitler finally accepted that it was all over, that there were no armies left that could come to his rescue, and decided to commit suicide rather than becoming a prisoner of war. But is that what really happened?

Secret FBI documents leaked

Hitler's death was often brought into question in the past, but it wasn't until secret FBI documents were leaked recently that this story really gained some momentum. According to these documents, it seems that neither Adolf Hitler nor Eva Braun committed suicide, but instead fled the country, with the assistance of Allen Dulles, Head of the U.S. OSS.

The Nazi leader allegedly used a submarine to take those closest to him to the coast of Argentina. Upon arrival, he found a new home at the foothills of the Andes. But even if he was able to escape, how did the FBI come to know about all of this?

The mysterious informant

As early as August 1945, the FBI received an anonymous letter from someone offering the information in exchange for political asylum. The agents agreed to meet his demands if his information was valuable, but they were stunned by what this informant shared with them.

He told the agents that two submarines arrived at the Argentinean coast, carrying high German officials, including Hitler and Eva Braun. According to his testimony, the Argentinean government welcomed the Nazis and gave them sanctuary.

The informant also gave them a very believable description of the Nazi leader's physical features, and this was more than enough to convince some agents there was something to his story.

Despite these accounts, the FBI never started an official investigation. The documents and eyewitness' accounts kept piling up, but for whatever reason, it wasn't enough to trigger a real reaction.

Russia DNA tests

When Hitler allegedly committed suicide in 1945, his and the remains of Eva Braun were promptly moved to Russia. There, they remained hidden from the public scrutiny for a long time.

However, in 2009, Nicholas Bellantoni, an archaeologist, performed DNA testing on one of the recovered skull fragments. His findings were shocking. The DNA material did not match either that of Hitler or Eva Braun.

This, combined with some previous theories and concerns, really shook the foundations of everything that was believed to be factual about the fate of the Nazi leader. Was he actually allowed to leave Germany, and live out the rest of his days in peace surrounded by the beautiful landscape of the Andes?

What to believe?

Is it possible that one of the most powerful men in the world at that time still had enough influence, connections, and money to pull off a plan like this? It most certainly is. Despite the fact that Hitler and Nazi Germany were on their knees in 1945, the Nazi leaders still had a lot of influence, not to mention money, and it is completely conceivable that they could stage their own disappearance.

On the other hand, it was proven almost beyond any doubt that Hitler was a person that clearly had some serious mental issues. The end of the Third Reich and the realization that his "dream" would not be fulfilled could have easily made him commit suicide. Regardless of how fiendish his idea was, there is no doubt that Hitler truly believed in it and was fully committed to it.

The evidence is mostly based on the accounts of eyewitnesses, but we've had ample opportunity to hear about people who often "see" wanted criminals and fugitives everywhere once they start expecting to see them. This is not to say that these accounts were false, but it must be said that they are not necessarily true either.

The DNA findings, on the other hand, are very interesting. Since DNA is highly unlikely to "lie," the question is whether the remains did not match because Hitler died in Argentina or because they were brought to Russia and then switched out for unknown reasons.

Due to the time that has past, this is one of those theories that will probably never be answered with certainty, but it is definitely quite possible. After all, a number of high-ranking Nazi officers found their refuge in Argentina after the war, so it would be far from surprising that the Fuhrer himself joined them there.

Chapter 16 – Zionist Occupation Government and Other White Supremacy Conspiracy Theories

The Zionist Occupation Government, or ZOG, refers to the theory that Jewish people control the country, and that the formal government is simply a puppet regime. This conspiracy is almost entirely rooted in White Supremacy, and anti-Semite groups. There are many versions of this conspiracy, but at its foundation, those who believe in the existence of the Zionist Occupation Government believe that Jews run the media and are planning to seize the banks, and take over the world. One of the first mentions of the Zionist conspiracy came in 1903, when a small, short-lived Russian newspaper called *Znamya* published a series of articles titled *The Protocols of the Sessions of the World Alliance of Freemasons* and of the *Sages of Zion.*

The Zionist conspiracy can be linked to The New World Order, but with almost no credible proof, and its heavy roots in antisemitism, the existence of ZOG is highly questionable. Regardless of its validity, ZOG brings up a string of other anti-Semitist and White Supremacist conspiracies.

White genocide

White genocide is a conspiracy theory developed by white nationalists who believe mass immigration, integration, miscegenation, low fertility rates, and abortion are being encouraged and forced in predominantly white countries for the purpose of making Caucasians a minority. This is another theory that is rooted in prejudice and heeds almost no credible proof.

Eugenics

While the practice of Eugenics is mostly tied to Nazi Germany, it originated in the United States years before World War II. The foundation of Eugenics was developed by Sir Francis Galton in the 1800's. Galton studied the upper classes of

Britain. His research led him to believe that social positions were based on genetic makeup. He therefore came to the conclusion that humans could "improve" their own species through selective-breeding. In the early 1920's and 30's, Eugenics was widely accepted amongst the United States academic community. The highly controversial system advocated for the sterilization of "defective" people, such as the mentally ill, the "feeble-minded", and criminals. The practice would include legal, compulsory sterilization of patients in state mental institutions. Up until the 1970s, Native American women were warned that if they did not agree to sterilization, they would be denied welfare benefits for themselves and their children.

During World War II, Eugenics was in full swing in Nazi Germany. Adolf Hitler's regime implemented the forced sterilization of over 5,000 people per month. The purpose was to breed out anyone the Nazis saw as unfit in order to create Hitler's vision of the perfect Aryan race.

A practice like Eugenics would be considered horrific in the United States in this day and age, but there is no denying Eugenics was a real system developed and practiced in America. This part of American history is often left out of history books and lessons.

Chapter 17 – The Reptilian Elite and Anti-Human Conspiracies

One of the wildest, yet rampant conspiracy theories suggests an elite group of non-human entities are responsible for ruling the entire world. The entities, commonly referred to by conspiracy theorists as the Reptilian Elite, are said to be species of lizard-people with the ability to shape shift and embody the human form. Though this concept sounds extraordinarily ludicrous, it is widely accepted among a surprisingly large number of conspiracists. The theory was popularized by well-known sports reporter turned professional conspiracy theorist, David Icke. Born and raised in Leicester, England, Icke grew up playing sports, eventually turning it into a career in his young adult years. When rheumatoid arthritis prevented him from participating in sports, Icke turned to broadcasting where he gradually climbed the professional ladder at the BBC network. In the late 80's, Icke took an interest in the Green Party. After being fired from the BBC for issues regarding his taxes, Icke moved on to politics, becoming a prominent leader for the Green Party. During this time, Icke explained that he began feeling a "presence" around him. The indescribable feeling led Icke to Peru where he experienced a spiritual awakening and subsequently made the decision to quit politics upon his return to England. In 1991, he made a highly controversial television appearance where he publicly announced that an incorporeal source was channeling him warnings of impending doom and natural devastation. Icke was met with mass criticism and ridicule, but eventually moved past the negativity. In 1998, Icke wrote and published The Biggest Secret, a book detailing his ideas behind the theory, including interviews with two British people claiming the royal family was, indeed, reptiles.

According to Icke, the Reptilians have reigned over humankind since the ancient times. Among them are all of the world's most powerful, influential, and recognizable people. Icke named Queen Elizabeth, George W. Bush, Bill and Hillary Clinton, Bob Hope, and Henry Kissinger as part of the cold-blooded empire, as well as countless other world leaders, corporate executives, Oscar winning actors, Grammy winning musicians, and other notable people.

David Icke believes that, for almost all of its existence, humankind has been manipulated into being fearful and complacent through media, politics, and control over food, water, shelter, and supplies. Icke insists that the goal of the Reptilian Elite is to keep the human race enslaved, and does so through the monetary system and the concept of jobs. In many of his works, Icke details a theory that this ruling class strives to keep their bloodline "intact", often referring to the The Burkes Peerage and Baronetage, a genealogy resource that reveals that all 44 United States President can be linked to the European royal bloodline.

Of course, there is very little proof available to back up the supposed existence of the Reptilian Elite, but Icke does offer a number of scientific explanations. Since the human brain can only process a limited spectrum of light, sound, and other energies, Icke believes the ruling class is capable of processing more light, and uses this knowledge to fool humans into thinking that existence is limited to the 3D world we experience.

David Ickes also links the Reptilian Elite to the New World Order and the Illuminati. The concept of the Reptilian Elite has also seeped into pop culture - the popular 1988 satirical action film, *They Live*. The film, starring Roddy Piper, Keith David, and Meg Foster, tells the tale of a nameless man who stumbles upon the existence of a ruling class of alien-like people who disguise themselves as human. This non-human ruling class manipulates people into spending money, breeding, and accepting the status quo set for them through subliminal messages in the media. The film quickly developed a cult following and continues to be referenced in media, clothing, and other public outlets today. Of course, the film was meant to be humorous, but many people joke that, "They Live is a documentary".

Chapter 18 – Craziest Conspiracy Theories That Never Happened

After looking at some of the biggest, most severe, and widely spread conspiracy theories, let us take a stroll down memory lane and remember some of the biggest fears and conspiracies that people came up with in the past.

Most of these were based merely on an idea that wasn't backed up by any real proof but created quite a fuss, either globally or on a local level.

Y2K computer apocalypse

If you were old enough to use a computer in late 90's, then you must have heard about the Y2K hype. In case you haven't, it was the idea that everything in the world that was run by computers, and computers themselves would suddenly stop working across the globe on midnight of January 1, 2000.

The so-called Y2K bug was based on the notion that when the clock struck midnight on January 1, 2000, the date would read 01/01/00, which the system could interpret as the year 1900 instead of 2000. This kind of error could potentially cause very serious difficulties in system operations and lead to some major disasters.

The theory itself wasn't completely bogus. The applications that relied on dates to perform any type of serious calculations could easily have turned into a mess. The companies started testing the possible implications by moving the computers' internal clocks forward, and the results were often disturbing.

But the fact was that the Y2K bug could only influence a very specific segment of the IT sector. Everyone else would either experience minor, easy to resolve difficulties, or none whatsoever. Some work had to be done. That's a fact because programmers from the early days used shortcuts to save space, and implemented two-digit instead of four-digit dates. But were we really facing a global disaster that was only avoided thanks to work completed years ahead of time?

Many believe that it was all a big conspiracy created to disseminate panic among people. At the same time, the fixes and patches on the old system made computer companies some serious money.

While there is no doubt that the Y2K bug could have created some inconvenience for certain sectors, and perhaps even cause an accident or two, the global panic was most certainly exaggerated. First of all, the bug was noticed well ahead of time, and with so many people working to implement the fix on the all important systems, it was highly unlikely that anything horrible could happen. Secondly, it created a lot of panic among regular computer users who weren't at all likely to be affected by this bug in any serious way.

The Reptilian elite

As absurd as this theory may sound, there is actually a significant number of people who believe that alien reptiles are living in our midst, masking themselves as humans, and plotting to turn the human race into their slaves. Reptilians have infiltrated all parts of our society, and are now some of the most powerful figures in the world.

From politicians and corporate executives to actors and singers, they are everywhere. All the horrible events in the world, like bloody wars, the Holocaust, terrorist attacks, and so forth are their doing.

The Reptilians (or "Annanuki," as some call them) have been controlling the human race since the earliest years of our civilization. The word "Annanuki" comes from ancient Mesopotamia, where the term was used to describe the children of their chief deity.

This is by far one of the wildest conspiracy theories described in this book, but, as mentioned, the number of believers is not insignificant.

The lost time conspiracy

If someone were to tell you, you were living in the year 1713, what would you tell them? But as crazy as this idea may sound, there was a German Historian, who claimed exactly this.

Heribert Illig took notice that the archaeological evidence from the period between the years 614 and 911 was very scarce. I don't want to say that he jumped to a conclusion, but he literally jumped to a conclusion that this is because those 300 years never really happened, and that we are being lied to about the period we live in (for whatever reason).

The theory was quickly disputed by science, particularly astronomy, since certain cosmic events take place at fixed intervals. One such event, the occurrence of Halley's comet, easily disputes Illig's claims, but the man definitely deserves brownie points for imagination.

There is no moon

Wait, what? This idea is neck to neck with the Reptilians, but there is a group of conspiracy theorists who claim that the moon doesn't exist.

Not believing in the moon landing is one thing, and we've devoted an entire chapter of this book to looking at some facts, evidence, and theories regarding this topic, but how on Earth can someone try to deny the existence of the Moon altogether?

This (thankfully) small group of people maintains that the Moon is just a hologram placed in the sky to do something. Of course, not even they can explain who placed it there or the reason for it, which further adds to its unlikelihood of being true.

CERN is trying to bring back Osiris

With some of these theories, I can see how an individual would come to believe them, but how he could get even a single person to believe their story remains a mystery. According to this conspiracy theory, CERN's Large Hadron Collider (LHC) is, in fact, an underground laboratory built to bring back the ancient Egyptian god Osiris.

Just like the Moon theory, this one is pretty random. As the proof of their claims, conspiracy theorists put forth the statue of Hindu god Shiva located at the entrance to the laboratory. The only connection between these two is that both are gods, but that's where it stops. There is nothing that links Osiris and Shiva.

Not that it would matter anyway, but it is funny to see what kind of "proof" some of these theories try to use to explain their claims.

The television controls our minds

It would seem that some 15% of Americans believe that their minds are being controlled through watching television. Talking about conspiracy theories, one can hardly get more paranoid than this. Imagine believing that every time you watch the TV, your mind is being influenced by the signals.

The belief is loosely based on the research by Herbert Krugman conducted in 1969. Krugman discovered that after a minute of watching television, a person's brain switches off the logical Beta waves, and instead moves to Alpha waves. During the entire time spent watching television, the brain is in "Alpha mode."

This created a fear that the mass media could be used to control our thoughts through special programs aimed at changing our behavioral patterns or belief systems. If our brain truly switches to Alpha waves while watching television, then it is not inconceivable that our minds would be more predisposed to accepting certain ideas and suggestions without rationally thinking them through. This theory also brought to light theories of subliminal messages in advertising, and even the idea that the government places small cameras and microphones inside televisions in order to spy on us. Of course, these are merely speculations of conspiracy theorists, as there is no firm evidence of any kind to back up these claims.

New diseases are invented by pharmaceutical companies to boost profits

This theory doesn't seem that outlandish at all. Big pharmaceutical companies survive on illness, diseases, and selling medications. At the same time, they have the resources, technology, and knowledge to come up with new strains of different bacteria or viruses to boost their sales with an accompanying cure.

However, conspiracy theorists take this possibility to a whole new level, claiming that these companies spend most of their time doing exactly this: coming up with new diseases for which they could sell the medications later on.

One incredibly rampant theory is that the government teamed up with the pharmaceutical industry to create the AIDS virus. When the illness first surfaced, it was predominantly infecting gay men and intravenous drug users. Conspiracy theorists believe AIDS was purposely spread through these demographics in order to "wipe them out". After the supposed plan failed, and AIDS began spreading throughout the entirety of the population, the pharmaceutical industry created drugs to treat the virus in order to profit off the mistake. It is even said a cure for AIDS has been discovered, but is being withheld from the public in order for big pharma to profit off overpriced treatments. While it is not impossible or beyond belief that pharmaceutical companies might be doing something shady in this regard (in fact, they probably are), it is quite unlikely that their main modus operandi is: create the disease, make the cure, sell the cure, rinse and repeat.

Airplanes exhaust dangerous chemicals in the air

Unlike the previous one, this theory is really out there. As discussed previously, there is a decent number of people believing this to be true or at least possible. Namely, that the trace left by airplanes while flying through the air is not simply the engine exhaust but rather a dangerous chemical sprayed under directions from the government.

So, those believing in this conspiracy theory are convinced that the government is deliberately poisoning its people without any particular reason or a goal.

One good way to look at the validity of conspiracy theories is to ask the question "why?" If something is being said with limited reasoning or because the person has malicious intent, then in all likelihood it is just complete and utter nonsense. It is one thing to believe that the USA came up with a fictional enemy to get their hands on the Middle Eastern oil, and completely different to think you are being poisoned just because those in power feel like it.

And on top of that, the airplane exhaust is something that actually exists.

The Bigfoot

We could hardly write a book about conspiracy theories without mentioning Bigfoot. There are a lot of people out there who believe that Bigfoot is real, and he is the missing link in our evolution. Once again, there is the idea that it is being kept from us for some strange, undefined reason.

Kurt Cobain was murdered

Nirvana fans around the world were outraged by the death of Kurt Cobain, and in turn, many conspiracies developed around the case. Fans insisted that Kurt Cobain did not commit suicide, but was actually murdered. Theorists believed that his girlfriend, Courtney Love, was responsible for his death, going as far as to edit his suicide note, but this was very unlikely. The crime scene and police reports made it very apparent that Cobain took his own life.

The CIA helped spread crack cocaine in the USA

If you are not sure who did it, the CIA did it, right? Despite the fact that people are often very willing to blame everything and anything on the USA clandestine organization, as far as this theory goes, the claims do make some sense.

Crack cocaine took reign in the American cities' inner circles during the 1980's. According to conspiracy theorists, the CIA turned a blind eye to Nicaraguan drug traffickers because they used a large portion of their drug profits to fund the Contra army's efforts in that country.

These allegations were, of course, completely disputed by the government, but true or not, it's not like those involved would actually admit to any wrongdoing in this matter. While there is no real evidence to back up these allegations, it is somewhat hard to believe that all of this was happening, and the government, the CIA, and the police were all powerless to do anything about it until it was too late.

Barack Obama is the Antichrist

We will conclude this section of unbelievable or lesser-known conspiracy theories with the one claiming that President Barack Obama is, in fact, the Antichrist himself. Apart from political motivation and difference in views, what prompted these people to believe this is beyond my comprehension. But, there you have it.

Chapter 19 – Craziest Conspiracy Theories That Did Happen

There are many conspiracy theories conceived and thought up that are outlandish and unbelievable, but on the contrary, there are some conspiracy theories that have been proven to be 100% true. Here are the most notable cases of seemingly outrageous theories turning out to be correct.

Big auto killed the electric car

Around the end of World War I, electric railways accounted for nearly 90% of transportation. At that time, the railways were very lucrative and cost cities very little to maintain. Railways were reliable, and allowed the everyday worker to easily commute to and from work without having to invest in a vehicle and the other host of costs that come with one. In this day, cars were seen as a novelty, and typically only owned by the upper-class as glorified toys. It seemed as though everybody was winning; everyone, except for a small number of very wealthy people who had overestimated the need for automobiles.

After losing over $65 million in one year, General Motors decided to take the initiative, rather than to come to terms with the loss. In the 1930s, General Motors, Firestone, and Goodyear teamed up with numerous oil companies. The companies united under the guise of multiple fake railway companies, buying out railways for the purpose of destroying them in order to make automobiles a necessity. By the 1950s, 900 of 1,200 railway systems were replaced with gas-fueled bus systems.

Though the ten companies involved were convicted of conspiracy in 1947, they managed to survive as their illegal monopoly became one of the most successful businesses in the world.

The government planned to get rid of Martin Luther King Jr.

As Martin Luther King Jr. rose to power as one of the most influential Civil Rights leaders in history, the FBI began seeing King as a threat. It is unclear whether the reason behind the FBI's suspicion was the product of straight-forward racism or fear of a revolution, but, unbeknownst to the public, the government marked Martin Luther King Jr. as an official enemy of the state.

Following his famous "I Have a Dream" speech, a memo circulating around FBI headquarters pronounced King as the "most dangerous and effective Negro leader in the country." Later memos spoke of, "neutralizing King as an effective Negro leader." Upon FBI wire-tapping of King, officials discovered he was involved in an extra-marital affair. The FBI used this information as blackmail, sending a letter threatening to reveal his affair if he did not take his own life.

Of course, Martin Luther King Jr. wound up being assassinated by James Earl Ray who is said to be an entirely separate entity from the government, but with a story as crazy as this one, it is difficult not to wonder if the assassination was planned.

The Watergate scandal

One of the most infamous conspiracies that actually happened is the Watergate scandal. In the 1970's, President Richard Nixon was tied to a crime that involved the FBI and CIA breaking in the Democratic National Committee building, and presidential candidate, George McGovern's personal office. During the break in, phone lines were tapped by Nixon's administration, and classified paperwork was stolen. Following the capture of the burglars, Nixon attempted to pay them off in order to keep them quiet about the crime.

Though the Nixon administration did everything they could to cover-up the scandal, Nixon's involvement in the crime eventually came to light. On August 9th, 1974, Richard Nixon chose to resign from the presidency rather than be impeached.

Though it was the most publicized, the Watergate scandal was not Nixon's only wrongdoing. His ongoing, hostile relationship with journalist and critic, Jack Anderson, came to a head when Nixon developed a plan to have him assassinated. Nixon employed two of his helpers to survey Anderson and his family, but before finalizing a plan to kill him, the helpers were pulled off the job, to instead, carry out the Democratic National committee building break in.

There was once a Soviet spy in Congress

In the 1950s, Joe McCarthy's infamous communist witch hunt had the nation on edge. Ironically, only years before, a supposed New York Democrat named Samuel Dickstein was an active member of the United States Congress. Dickstein was even responsible for the creation of the House Committee of Un-American Activities, the committee that would later be in charge of hunting down communists. Samuel Dickstein however, had been hired by what is now known as the KGB to gather information on the United States government and report back to the Soviets.

Dickstein's participation in the treason was solely motivated by money. He had previously spied for both Poland and Britain for the same reason. Somehow, Dickstein was never indicted for his repeated treason, and later served for the New York Supreme Court. There is even a plaza named after Samuel Dickstein in Lower East Side Manhattan.

One of America's deadliest massacres was covered up for years

In early 1920's Tulsa, Oklahoma, a young black man named Dick Rowland accidently tripped and fell into a white women named Sarah Page. During this era, racism was rampant and Rowland was subsequently arrested for his innocent slip up. The following day, a lynch mob arrived at the prison where Dick Rowland was being held with clear intent to murder the man. A black mob also showed up at the prison in order to protect Rowland. In an unexpected turn of events, a single gunshot marked the beginning of a 16-hour race riot that left

39 people dead. Afterward, the entire city of Tulsa was in shambles, and two black hospitals were completely destroyed, as well as the area referred to as "Black Wall Street", a place populated by affluent African-Americans.

The tragedy was immediately covered up and forgotten by the city's inhabitants. The dead were reportedly thrown in mass graves, coal mines, or the Arkansas River. Years later, a shocking, in-depth investigation of the riot was performed. The research brought to light over 260 more deaths than were originally recorded. This information classified the Tulsa Race Riot as "the worst single act of domestic violence on U.S. soil since the Civil War", yet almost no one has heard of the incident.

Tuskegee syphilis experiment

From 1932 through 1972, the United States conducted an experiment that involved nearly 400 African American males that were unaware of their participation in the study. The experiment sought to see if the STI, syphilis, affected African American men differently than it affected white men. Over the course of 40 years, black men that were infected with syphilis were told they had "bad blood", rather than the truth, and were not provided with treatment. By the time the study concluded, only 74 of the nonconsenting participants survived.

Project MK-ULTRA

In 1953, Central Intelligence Agency director, Allen Dulles, authorized a covert operation that would involve the use of mind-altering drugs and substances on unwitting participants. The highly invasive program was developed when Dulles discovered that a number of American prisoners had been subject to "mind control" techniques in Korea. Project MK-ULTRA had many purposes. One purpose was to develop a truth serum for more effective interrogations of enemies, another purpose was to develop an "amnesia pill" that made agents immune to mind-control techniques performed by enemies, another was to develop a type of programmable assassin, or "Manchurian Candidate", and finally they set out to control the minds of high-profile enemies such as Fidel Castro.

Along with the secret administration of drugs, project MK-ULTRA utilized radiological implants, hypnosis and subliminal persuasion, electroshock therapy, and isolation techniques. Using research as a front, LSD was secretly administered to CIA employees, U.S. soldiers, the institutionalized, and even the general public.

Frank Olson, a 43-year-old civilian germ-warfare researcher was subjected to the experiment during a meeting with the head of Project MK ULTRA. Olson, along with four other scientists, had their drinks spiked by the CIA with acid and were informed of this 20 minutes after they'd already been drugged. Frank Olson experienced severe adverse reactions to the drug, and was later reported to have hurled himself out of the 10th floor window of a New York hotel room.

The CIA ceased further experimentation with the drug, concluding it was far too unpredictable to produce reliable research, but the agency still saw repercussions from MK-ULTRA nearly twenty years later. When information about the experimental program leaked, Frank Olson's family learned he'd been unsuspectedly drugged by the agency. President Gerald Ford insisted that the Olson family be paid $750,00, but upon exhuming Olson's body in the 1990's, it was discovered that he may have actually died of blunt force trauma to the head received before his deadly fall.

Along with Olson, a tennis player who was subjected to the CIA's program fell into a coma and died after receiving a derivative of mescaline. Project MK-ULTRA is likely to have caused many other deaths, but records of the tests were destroyed in 1973. This was most likely to prevent further lawsuits from families of the victims.

Alcohol was poisoned during prohibition

During the 1920s, Prohibition enforced a ban on drinking alcohol. The ban was met with much adversity, and many illegal bars, referred to as speakeasies, opened up in cities all over the country. People would go to speakeasies in secret to drink and mingle, just like anyone would in a legal bar today. During the Prohibition era, the government would shut down speakeasies and seize alcohol whenever one was found out, but when drinking remained a rampant activity despite the ban, government officials became very frustrated.

While it was common for people to experience alcohol poisoning due to bootlegged whiskies and fake gins during this era, the government upped the ante and ordered the poisoning of all industrial alcohols manufactured within the United States. Speakeasy owners and bootleggers were known to steal these alcohols and re-sell them as drinkable, so it was guaranteed the poisoned supply would circulate around speakeasies. The purpose of the poisoning was to scare people out of drinking, but the poison program ended up killing upwards of 10,000 people.

The idea of alcohol being banned in this day and age sounds preposterous, but imagine all of the other substances that are currently illegal, such as marijuana. You have to wonder if the government continues to employ poison programs such as this one.

Operation Northwoods

During the time of the Cold War, the United States began planning fake attacks on America that were to be blamed on Cuba. The purpose for these fake attacks was to garner support from American citizens for the war against the Latin American communist country. Though the operation never surpassed its planning stages, this is something to consider when terrorist attacks take place here in America and blame is placed on current enemies.

The NSA illegally spies on its own citizens

In 2005, reports began surfacing that the National Security Agency, or the NSA had been illegally intercepting communications between millions of ordinary American citizens. When the information surfaced, the government attributed the data collection to the prevention of terrorist attacks. Citizens accepted this explanation, but by 2014, it was discovered that nearly 90% of information being collected by the NSA was from American citizens with absolutely no ties to terrorist activity. According to the American Civil Liberties Union, the NSA was in clear violation of the Fourth Amendment and is currently pursuing a lawsuit against the security agency.

Conspiracies such as this used to be a thing of fiction, portrayed only in movies and novels such as George Orwell's, *1984*, but now it is a fact that Americans are indeed being spied on. What could be the purpose of this?

Chapter 20 – Miscellaneous Conspiracy Theories

In modern days, new conspiracy theories are constantly being discovered and reported through mass media, television and the especially, the internet. It is impossible to cover every conspiracy theory that circulates today, but here is a collection of interesting theories that don't fit into any particular category aforementioned in this book.

The Denver International Airport is actually an underground military bunker

In 1995, construction of the Denver International Airport was met by much suspicion from residents of Colorado. Since a fully-functional, technologically up to date airport already existed in Denver, it was unclear why a second airport in the city was necessary. Regardless, construction continued and upon completion it was noted that the airport housed an incredible amount of unoccupied space.

Conspiracy theorists believe this space was built to cover up an underground military bunker that is meant to house the country's most important people in the event of an attack. Evidence of this theory lies in the exceedingly bizarre and terrifying art pieces on the walls that depict mass genocide. A stone in the airport's terminal thanks The New World Airport Commission for funding the creation of the airport, but upon further investigation, it was discovered that The New World Airport Commission is an organization that does not exist.

Big pharma aims to keep people sick

Many conspiracy theorists believe that the pharmaceutical industry aims to keep people sick so that they can continuously profit off drugs. As many lifesaving drugs are outrageously priced, this theory is not terribly outlandish.

An upsurge in the use of psychiatric drugs in recent years really brought this conspiracy to light. Millions of Americans have been diagnosed with mental disorders ranging from depression, to anxiety, to ADD and are currently being heavily medicated for these issues. Rather than exploring natural solutions or relief, doctors are quick to prescribe anti-depressants, anti-psychotics, and stimulants that are meant for long-term use. When a person is prescribed an anti-depressant, it is likely they will be on a form of medication for life, meaning long-term profits for big pharma. Conspiracists also believe the pharmaceutical companies withhold cures for various diseases in order to continue profiting off treatments.

Fluoride in the water supply is meant for mind control

Water in the United States is fluoridated for health reasons, one of which is to prevent tooth decay. The U.S. is not alone in its fluoridation of the water supply. Still, very few countries practice this. The lack of participation of other countries in the fluoridation of the water supply has led some conspiracy theorists to speculate that fluoride acts as some sort of mind control agent. There is proof regarding this theory.

Paul McCartney is dead

Conspiracy theorists and Beatles fans have insisted since 1966 that Paul McCartney is actually dead. While the origin of the conspiracy is unclear, it continues to be perpetuated by Beatles fans to this day. Many theorists believe McCartney was replaced by a lookalike named William Shears Campbell. Billy Shears is also the name of the fictional leader of Sgt. Pepper's Lonely Hearts Club Band. Some fans believe the remaining members of the Beatles named the character as a sign. Theorists point out other symbols in The Beatles memorabilia and music, such as the cover of the famed Abbey Road album. The iconic cover photo captures The Beatles crossing the street. Each member is wearing shoes in the picture, except McCartney.

In the song "I'm So Tired", a portion of lyrics played backwards seem to say "Paul is dead, man. Miss him! Miss him!" Other symbolism in the Beatles' lyrics and imagery is also said to "prove" that Paul McCartney is dead, but no DNA or forensic evidence backs this theory up. It is likely that the rumor was started by fans and circulated back to the band. The Beatles were notorious for their ambiguity and probably used the knowledge of this conspiracy theory to generate more mystery around the band.

The CIA killed Michael Jackson

In 2009, the King of Pop passed away unexpectedly in Los Angeles, CA. His death was met by sadness and suspicion from many fans around the globe. Conspiracy theorists believe that the CIA was responsible for murdering Michael Jackson due to his plans to warn the world of an upcoming, mass genocide. It was rumored that Jackson had signed a contract with Sheikh Abdullah bin Hamad al-Khalifa that stated, in exchange for millions of dollars, the singer would be permitted to use his series of sold-out United Kingdom concerts to heed this warning to his masses of fans.

It is said that Michael Jackson's, "We've Had Enough" is a song about innocent Palestinians being slaughtered by Israeli Defense Forces. According to conspiracy theorists, Sheikh Abdullah bin Hamad al-Khalifa loaned Michael Jackson the millions required to fund the tour, and Jackson's repayment was to expose Israel's abuse of the Palestinian people.

Data transmitted by a Russian Military's Kosmos 2450 satellite shows that immediately before Jackson's death, electromagnetic pulses consistent with the pattern of EMR weapons were present in the exact location of the pop singer's home. The events leading up to his death, as well as the data from Russian Intelligence officials led many theorists to believe Jackson was assassinated by the CIA.

Princess Diana was murdered

In 1997, Princess Diana and her boyfriend, Dodi Fayed were killed in a fatal car wreck in Paris. The untimely passing of the princess threw the global media into a frenzy. The car wreck was said to have been caused by invasive paparazzi chasing the limousine that Diana was riding in. Though both French and

British authorities ruled Princess Diana's death an accident, conspiracy theorists believe her death was planned. It is rumored that the fatal crash was arranged by British Special Forces who were working in conjunction with the Royal Family. Theorists believe that Princess Diana was murdered in order to prevent her from revealing embarrassing secrets about her former husband, Prince Charles, and other members of the Royal family.

TWA Flight 800

In 1996, TWA Flight 800 crashed just off the coast of Long Island, New York, killing all 230 passengers on board. According to the National Transportation Safety Board, the fatal crash was caused by a gas tank explosion, but eyewitness accounts tell a different story. Those who'd witnessed the crash claimed to have seen a fiery streak fly directly at the plane right before it crashed. A documentary aired on EPIX argued proof of external detonation, but most theories point to a missile launched by a terrorist organization, or possibly, the U.S. Navy. These theories have been fervently denied by government officials, but if something out of the ordinary did happen, it is likely that a cover up ensued.

Life exists on Mars

In 1976, photos taken by NASA's Viking orbiter gave many conspiracy theorists the idea that life exists on Mars. Celebrity comedian, Richard Belzer details this theory in his popular book, UFOs, JFK, and Elvis: You Don't Have to be Crazy to Believe. Belzer describes the 1976 photos as featuring a gigantic, sculpted face on the surface of the planet, as well as a sphinx, and a five-sided pyramid. While this so-called, photographic evidence seems a bit over the top, recent studies have discovered very viable proof of water on mars. NASA's Mars Reconnaissance Orbiter used an imaging spectrometer to reveal signs of hydrated minerals on the planet. Hydrated minerals could mean there is water on Mars, and finding water on Mars will likely lead to the first discovery of life in outer space.

Global warming is a myth

Many conspiracy theorists believe the idea of global warming, or climate change, was forced into heads of the general public in order for the government to inflict higher taxes, control our lifestyles, and develop a totalitarian government. Though there is an incredible amount of evidence that proves man-made climate change is a very real threat to our society, those who don't believe in global warming argue that the rise in temperature has actually leveled off since the year 1998.

Shakespeare did not actually write any of his plays

As very little information is available on William Shakespeare's personal history, many conspiracy theorists argue that the famed playwright did not, in fact, write a single one of his historical plays. What little biographical information that has been discovered on William Shakespeare simply confirms that he was a businessman and a minor stage actor. The anti-Shakespeare crowd believes this background says that he would not have been nearly intelligent enough to write the plays on his own, but just smart enough to pass them off as his own. Conspiracy theorists believe more likely candidates for the creation of Shakespeare's work are Francis Bacon, Ben Jonson, Sir Walter Raleigh, or Christopher Marlowe.

Chapter 21 – Conspiracy Theories vs. Mass Media

After reviewing some crazy and some not so crazy conspiracy theories, the question one must ask themselves is where to draw the line. At what point does a conspiracy theory become a real possibility, a real alternative to what the mass media are serving us?

The fact is that some conspiracy theories have actually provided results and forced to light some new evidence in many cases, where this would not be possible if people decided to believe the media blindly. On the other hand, there are those, as we've seen, which created a lot of fuss without a real reason behind it, and resulted in nothing else but some panic among the people.

One thing I can certainly suggest is always to question the mainstream media. It is a sad fact that the media is often used as a weapon controlled by those in power and as such will share the information which doesn't necessarily have to be true.

A healthy dose of skepticism is more than welcome in today's day and age. The information we are being served, often s comes from unreliable or influenced sources and is manipulated in order to achieve a particular agenda. No one will think you are crazy if you refuse to take things for granted and seek more evidence before accepting something as a fact.

The important thing is to stay objective and reasonable in this quest. As you can see, some people just take things way too far, to the point where no sane person can accept their skepticism as healthy. Denying the existence of the Moon or believing that we live in a society governed by reptiles certainly belong to this category.

Focus your efforts on things that really matter, instead. Questioning the decisions of your government and looking for reasons behind certain actions is a good thing. It may get you in trouble, especially if you start poking in the wrong place, but in the grand scheme of things it is beneficial to everyone.

There is a fine line between looking for the truth and seeking out conspiracies for their own sake. Truth seekers go after something they care about or something they believe is truly important. Conspiracy theorists just look for an excuse to challenge what is being presented to them, even when there is no evidence to support their claims.

Of course, certain conspiracy theories can be fun, even if they are silly or ludicrous. There is nothing wrong with pursuing those to an extent as well since there is usually at least some truth to most of them. Just don't allow them to become your preoccupation. Take them for what they are, a fun pastime that may lead to an interesting discovery, also don't let them take up too much time or space in your life.

As for the media, do not let a single source become your primary source of information. As mentioned before, it happens far too often that a certain source of information becomes tainted due to certain political or other interests of those in power, and then the information that you hear can become thwarted and unreliable. Always keep your options open, look for the information wherever you can get it, and then make your own decisions and judgments about things. This is the only way to protect yourself from being fed misinformation and half-truths.

Conclusion

Although theories are, in essence, unproven speculations, the stories you just finished reading hopefully made you more skeptical about what the media is peddling. Even though most of the stories seemed like they came straight out of a horror movie, the intent is not to scare you; it is actually the opposite.

Conspiracy theories aim to make people question what popular media says is "the truth." I hope that after reading about the most pertinent conspiracy theories, you are now more skeptical than and not as easy to fool as you were before.

Again, the aim of this book is not to turn people into paranoid, nervous wrecks; just into more skeptical ones; and what the world really needs right now are more critical thinkers.

***

Stay up to date on the latest news, free promotions and much more!

http://bit.ly/CS_bookclub

Thank you for reading to the end!

***

56491486R00064

Made in the USA
San Bernardino, CA
12 November 2017